THE BRIEF HISTORY OF
LANCASHIRE

THE BRIEF HISTORY OF
LANCASHIRE

STEPHEN DUXBURY

First published 2011

The History Press
The Mill, Brimscombe Port
Stroud, Gloucestershire, GL5 2QG
www.thehistorypress.co.uk

British Library Cataloguing in Publication Data.
A catalogue record for this book is available from the British Library.

ISBN 978 0 7524 6288 2

Typesetting and origination by The History Press
Printed in Great Britain

CONTENTS

Introduction   6

1. A Brief History of Lancashire, BC   7

2. Romans, Anglo-Saxons and Vikings, AD 1 to 1066   17

3. Normans, Angevins, Plantagenets
   and Wars of the Roses, 1066-1485   31

4. Tudors, Stuarts and the Civil Wars, 1485-1688   50

5. William and Mary, the Hanoverians
   and the '15 and '45 Rebellions, 1688-1745   86

6. The Reform Act, the Repeal of the Corn Laws,
   Literary Lancashire and the Nineteenth Century   100

7. The Cotton Industry and its Inventors   119

8. Industry, Transport and Population   153

9. Modern Times, Mid-Nineteenth Century to 1945   168

Bibliography   179

Index   182

INTRODUCTION

I have always been a proud Nelsoner and a proud Lancastrian, a pride which has probably been enhanced by my
forty-year exile in Kent, during which time I developed
a desire to learn as much as I could about my hometown,
home-county and family history. As a result of my researches
I amassed a collection of over 200 Lancashire books and
booklets, together with a mass of information relating to and
peripheral to my family history. This information includes
stories and histories that interested and intrigued me, and
I have long felt the need to share them with a wider audience,
hence this book.

My intention is to present a history of Lancashire in a
national context, as well as a local one, detailing the significant role played by Lancashire and Lancastrians in
the history of England. My aim is to produce a book that
all proud Lancastrians will want to read and have on their
bookshelves.

Steve Duxbury,
Kent, 2011

CHAPTER ONE

A BRIEF HISTORY OF LANCASHIRE, BC

THE BIG BANG

It would have been most appropriate if the person who coined the expression 'The Big Bang' had been born in Lancashire, since the history of Lancashire begins with the Big Bang, but he was not. Sir Fred Hoyle was a Yorkshireman, born in Bingley. I do wish that it had been otherwise. It might be claimed that it is typical of a Yorkshireman to do things with a Big Bang, compared with we Lancastrians, who tend to be more refined, but that is to ignore the fact that many Lancastrians, myself included, have Yorkshire blood in their veins. I once read that, at the 1851 Census, 25 per cent of the population of Lancashire had been born outside the county, Ireland and Yorkshire being large contributors to the stream of migrants, so I will refrain from mocking the good residents of Yorkshire.

I would point out two things about the expression 'the Big Bang', however. Firstly, Sir Fred coined the phrase as a derisory comment on the theory that the universe rapidly expanded from a minute point, a singularity, to the size that we see today. He could not believe that the universe started with a Big Bang, and favoured the Steady State Theory, which says that the universe is constant and stable, with new matter being generated to fill the void created by the expansion of the universe. Derisory or not, the phrase caught on.

The second point is that diagrams of the Big Bang, showing a huge explosion and outwards spherical expansion of the universe, are misleading. Since time and space was created inside the expanding universe, there is no point outside the universe from which an observer could watch the Big Bang, and there was no medium outside the universe that could convey the sound of the Big Bang to the ears of an observer.

Moving rapidly on, in 1929 Edwin Hubble, an American, demonstrated that almost every galaxy in the universe is moving away from every other galaxy, and the farther away from us a galaxy is the faster it is moving away from us. The inference is that, if we reverse this expansion and look back into history, all galaxies started from the same point of origin – the singularity. The expansion of the universe from the singularity would have started with the Big Bang, some 13.7 billion years ago.

ECHOES OF THE BIG BANG

In 1965, Arno Penzias and Robert Wilson, two scientists researching satellite communications at Bell Laboratories in the USA, picked up some interference in their microwave receiver that they could not explain. The interference came from all directions and they could not identify its source. It turned out that they had accidentally discovered the echo from the Big Bang, microwave background radiation that bathed the whole universe, providing further corroboration of the Big Bang theory. The temperature of this radiation was a mere 2.7 degrees Kelvin above absolute zero.

RIPPLES IN SPACE

Scientists investigated the microwave background radiation in more depth, first by high-flying balloons and more recently by satellite-born instruments. They found that the radiation was not quite uniformly distributed, but was a patchwork of areas that were fractionally lower in temperature than adjacent areas. These tiny ripples or variations in temperature had existed since the Big Bang, and, as the universe expanded, were responsible for the coalescence of gasses into clumps which gradually formed the galaxies. Gravitational forces caused the gasses inside the galaxies to condense into stars, many of which were huge, much larger and much hotter than our own sun. The pressures and temperatures inside these huge stars were so enormous that a process which built heavier elements from lighter ones was able to take place, a process which itself generated huge amounts of energy. Thus, hydrogen was converted to helium, helium to carbon, and so on.

THE DEATH OF A STAR, THE BIRTH OF A PLANET

Our own galaxy, the Milky Way, is a spiral galaxy. It would take a space ship, travelling at the speed of light, 100,000 years to cross the Milky Way galaxy. Our sun, being relatively small, is only able to convert hydrogen into helium, so all the other heavier elements in the universe, indeed, the heavier elements that make up our own bodies, and Lancashire, and the world we live in, were generated not inside our own sun but in some long-expired giant star. After burning for perhaps billions of years, the giant star would begin to run out of nuclear fuel. Most of the hydrogen in the star would have been converted to helium, and so on. It was this conversion that generated the energy to enable the star to withstand the enormous gravitational pull of the mass of the star and keep it from collapsing in on itself. Once the supply of nuclear fuel approached exhaustion, the star would begin to collapse under its own gravity. The inwards collapse of the star would be matched by a huge outward explosion, a supernova, as the gaseous outer shell of the star was blasted off into space. The remains of the star would continue to collapse in on itself until it became a white dwarf star, a fraction of the size of the original giant star, but consisting of hugely compressed matter, a teaspoonful of which would weigh an enormous amount in earthly terms. Our own sun was formed some 5 billion years ago from the gaseous leftovers of a supernova explosion.

Meanwhile, the vast amount of material blasted outwards from the dying star, including all the heavier elements generated within the megastar, slowly coalesced due to gravitational forces, into planet-sized objects, smaller objects merging together all the time to create larger objects. And so, some 4.6 billion years ago, our earth was born. The earth and its sister planets were caught by the gravitational attraction of our sun, forming the solar system, and the earth cooled and hardened, over time. Living organisms were already in existence on the earth some 3.5 billion years ago.

AND THEN IT RAINED, AND THE EARTH BREATHED AND SHIVERED

As the earth cooled, it rained. Well, I know that Lancastrians are used to rain, but this rain went on for eons as the moisture in the atmosphere condensed. Being a weather forecaster at the time would have been easy – rain, rain and more rain. The oceans were born and in time they filled with simple life. Some 2 billion years ago, algae-like organisms called Cyanophytes, also known as blue-greens, were dominant, and over a long period of time these blue-greens were responsible for generating the vast amount of oxygen in the atmosphere that makes the earth habitable. According to Paul Falkowski of Rutgers University, New Jersey, USA, this process developed as follows: 2.2 billion years ago cyanobacteria evolved that had the ability to use sunlight to generate oxygen from water. Then, 1.9 million years ago, an amoeba-like organism absorbed one of these cyanobacteria, by chance, and from this combination every tree, plant and seaweed on earth eventually evolved. Thus, from 1.9 million years ago onwards, the combined organism, and the organisms that developed from it, flourished and generated oxygen in steadily increasing quantities. Much of this oxygen was reabsorbed as these organisms died and decayed, but from 750 million years onwards the scale of development and reproduction of these organisms led to huge quantities of their remains accumulating on the sea bed or in marshland as the organisms died, locking enormous amounts of carbon into chalks, limestones and coal measures. This left free the large amounts of oxygen that would have otherwise been required to break down the dead organisms, had they not been converted into chalks, limestones and coal measures. The increase in the oxygen content of the air encouraged the development of animal life. The first plants colonised the land 475 million years ago and the first land animals emerged 400 million years ago.

The earth heaved up huge volcanic mountain ranges and, over time, the volcanic rocks of the earth were weathered into sediments which were deposited in the depths of the seas, forming new sedimentary rocks. As mentioned above, limestones were created in the depths of the seas from the shells and skeletons of creatures living and dying in the seas and coal measures were formed from the compacting of ancient vegetation on land. Sea beds were heaved up by tectonic movements in the earth's crust and became mountains, and eventually the geology of Lancashire emerged, as further described below.

An Ice Age began 1.8 million years ago and ended just 12,000 years ago, or so. During that time there were several glacial periods where the ice advanced over much of Lancashire and retreated again, the ice reaching its most recent peak 18,000 years ago. We might indeed be in an inter-glacial period now, destined to experience a further ice invasion in the future, global warming permitting. The ice and the huge amounts of melt-water and rainwater that went with it had a significant role to play in shaping modern Lancashire, both in terms of carving out valleys in the uplands and depositing the resultant material in the lowlands, as we shall see.

CONTINENTAL DRIFT

200 million years ago, there was only one continent, a huge one called Pangaea. If human beings had been around, with cars and motorways, they could have driven from Blackpool to Boston, Massachusetts, in a day. Then continental drift set in, as Pangaea broke up and the constituents of Pangaea, the earth's currently identifiable land masses, drifted away from each other. The speed of the drift was imperceptibly slow, but it was enough over 200 million years for the land masses to reach their present positions. (The land masses are still moving, by the way.)

THE DEVELOPMENT OF MAN

Although, as stated above, living organisms developed on the earth some 3.5 billion years ago, living creatures were confined in the seas until 400 million years ago. Life continued to evolve until the dinosaur era, but 65 million years ago, catastrophe struck – literally. A huge meteor is thought to have hit the earth, on the Yucatan Peninsula (now part of Mexico) in Central America. The shock of the collision and the change in the earth's climate caused by the blocking out of the sun's rays (as debris was thrown into the atmosphere by the collision) caused a mass extinction of life on earth, not the first mass extinction in the earth's history. The dinosaurs suffered badly and were wiped out over time.

Of the living creatures that survived the mass extinction, a species of small, shrew-like animal, our ancestor, appears to have succeeded in adapting and developing and filling the void left by the dinosaurs and other extinct species. By some 40 million years ago, this shrew-like species had evolved into species of monkeys, and, from these monkeys, apes evolved some 10 million years ago. Our ancestors, the hominids, evolved from the apes some 7 million years ago and began to walk upright some 4 million years ago. *Homo habilis* evolved, followed by *homo erectus*, until, some 100,000 years ago, genetic mixing and mutation created *homo sapiens.* Modern man, *homo sapiens sapiens,* evolved 40,000 years ago.

It has to be said that not much of this development, if any, happened in Lancashire, as far as I am aware. It happened in East Africa, from where our ancestors spread around the world. They were hunter-gatherers, nomadic wanderers, until 10,000 years ago, when they discovered agriculture and started growing crops and tending farm animals on a more settled basis, although there were still forces that caused them to migrate from time to time.

LANCASHIRE AS WE SEE IT

During the Ordovician geological period, some 450 million years ago, Lancashire was almost entirely covered by a shallow sea, off the continent of Europe, and over tens of millions of years a thick layer of mudstone was laid down in this shallow sea, its constituent materials having been washed from continental land masses by immense rivers. Volcanic activity followed as the Borrowdale Volcanic Series threw up the Lake District into a huge dome, baking existing rocks and introducing new volcanic ones. This activity created Lancashire's oldest rocks, the Silurian slate, limestone and grits of Higher Furness, as we see them today.

Some 350 million years ago, a deeper sea covered large areas of Northern England, and in this sea were deposited the shales, limestone and millstone grit of the Carboniferous period, the limestone being formed from the shells of sea creatures and the millstone grit from the sands washed into the sea by huge continental rivers. Again, during the Carboniferous period, the sea receded, such that a mass of vegetation was able to grow and decay into thick layers, forming the coal measures that have been so valuable to Lancashire. Generally, these limestones, millstone grits and coal measures were turned into rock deep underground by the enormous pressures exerted upon them as further deposits were laid over them.

Subsequent earth movements, some 270 million years ago, folded up the Carboniferous strata, and weathering over millions of years left us with the Pennines, as we see them, partly millstone grit, as in Pendle, Bowland and Rossendale, partly limestone, as in Ribblesdale, and partly coal measures, as in south-central Lancashire. The lowlands of south-west and west Lancashire are under-laid with marls and sandstones deposited in a huge basin created alongside the folded Carboniferous uplands during the Mesozoic period, over 200 million years ago. Large areas of lowland Lancashire were covered with peat and mosses, of geologically recent origin, resulting from long periods of vegetation growth in a damp environment. The mosses conceal the remains of trees, harking back to an era when most of the county was covered by forest.

And so geology, time and weather have left us with the Lancashire that we know, the uplands of Furness and the Pennines, the coalfields of south-central Lancashire and the Lancashire Plain in the south-west and west of the county, but there is yet another factor that affected our view of the county – glaciation.

GLACIATION

The results of glaciation on the county are more than cosmetic. During the last period of glaciation, which ended 12,000 years ago, only certain parts of Lancashire, such as the Furness peaks, Pendle and the higher parts of Rossendale, stood up above the ice. The ice cap was not stationary, but was moving, grinding the earth that lay beneath. Glaciers carved huge valleys, where previously there had been smaller ones. Meltwater carved out ravines such as that at Cliviger. The moving ice shifted vast amounts of earth debris and dumped it in the river valleys of the uplands and across the Lancashire Plain as a thick layer of boulder clay. There are rocks, called erratics, resting in Lowland Lancashire today that can be shown to have been transported from the mountains of Scotland and the Lake District. One large boulder found near Burscough Junction, for instance, had its origins in Scotland. Another erratic, the Great Stone of Fourstones, can be found at Lowgill, on the Yorkshire border, east of Lancaster. Without glaciation, Lancashire would look markedly different to the Lancashire that we see, today.

THE BIRTH OF LANCASTRIANS

Prior to the last glaciation, Neanderthal man (our ancestral relative but not our direct ancestor) was present in the southern half of England, but if any Neanderthals lived in Lancashire at that time (which is unlikely, especially since there were only around 15,000 Neanderthals in the whole of Europe), the evidence of their existence has been obliterated by the ice. Therefore, the human history of Lancashire effectively begins 12,000 years ago, with the last retreat of the ice. As the ice retreated, vegetation invaded the barren wilderness left behind, the vegetation was followed by animals and the animals were followed by humans.

For thousands of years, Lancashire was inhospitable and thinly populated. The earliest evidence of human activity comes from Poulton-le-Fylde, where an elk skeleton and two bone spear-points dating back to 10,000 BC were found. The bones bore signs of cut marks made by humans. Middle Stone Age humans appear to have been the first to populate Lancashire, albeit sparsely. They had their origin in the Mediterranean lands and used small, pigmy flints as weapons and tools. They were replaced by Neolithic humans of the New Stone Age, around 2,500 BC. These newcomers were characterised by better flint weapons and tools and a more sedentary existence, rearing domesticated animals and growing crops. They were the builders of burial mounds, or barrows, that can be seen atop many a Lancashire hill.

The Lancashire coastline at that time was further west than it is today. The sea has since encroached upon the land. Ancient animals used to forage along the muddy coast, followed by humans. Footprints of animals and humans dating back perhaps 5,000 years have been found in the hardened layers of mud exposed by the sea – around Formby, for instance. I found an animal footprint there myself in 2007. I believe that these footprints are of Stone-Age origin.

The Neolithic peoples were replaced by the Celts, who brought the Bronze Age to Lancashire around 2,000 BC, using flints in parallel with bronze. Given its scarcity, bronze was used for the more notable weapons and tools. The Celts were sedentary farmers but were also involved in trading. There was a trade route through the Ribble Valley and there is evidence that items of Irish origin were traded, not just local wares. An Early Bronze Age woodhenge dating back 3,000 years was found at Bleasdale, in Bowland. This large circle of tree trunks seems to have been a burial site, among other things, as burial urns have been excavated from the site.

The arrival of new tribes of Celts around 500 BC heralded the commencement of the Iron Age. Iron Age forts of Celtic origin can be found at Warton Crag, near Carnforth, the largest such fort in Lancashire, Castercliffe, above Nelson and Colne, Camp Hill, near Liverpool, Portfield, near Whalley, Castlestede, near Lancaster, Castlehead, near Lindale on the Cartmel Peninsula, and Skelmore Head, near Ulverston. There is evidence that circular roofed huts were once present in these forts.

During this period, Lancashire found itself subsumed into the tribal territory of the Brigantes, and was about to be absorbed into a much larger empire with the coming of the Romans.

CHAPTER TWO

ROMANS, ANGLO-SAXONS AND VIKINGS, AD 1 TO 1066

THE ROMANS

Julius Caesar came, saw and went away again. He certainly never reached Lancashire in his military expeditions of 55 BC and 54 BC. The closest he got was probably Wheathampstead, in Hertfordshire. But Britain's richness, at least its agricultural richness in the southern part of the country, was confirmed. It was left to the Emperor Claudius to take the next step and commence the invasion of Britain in AD 43. He was prompted by the increasing wealth and strength of the Celts, the possible threat they presented to Gaul and the potential mineral wealth possessed by the islands. The immediate spur was the death of Cunobelinus (Shakespeare's Cymbeline), King of the Trinovantes, of Essex and Suffolk. Cunobelinus' sons quarrelled over the succession, causing a request for help to go out to Rome.

The Romans' push northwards was delayed in AD 61 by the bloody rising led by Queen Boudica (commonly but incorrectly known as Boadicea) who led the Iceni tribe in the sacking of Roman veterans' colonies in Colchester, London and St Albans. The rebellion was put down, with even greater bloodshed, and by AD 71 the Romans had secured the enormous area south of a line from Lincoln, through Leicester,

*The standard of the White Horse: Saxon invaders, sandwiched between
the age of the Romans and the Vikings, carried this symbol at their head.*

Cirencester and Bath to Seaton on the south Devon coast.
Raids south by the Brigantes, perhaps coupled with the
promise of mineral wealth, convinced the Romans that the
North needed to be subdued. The Brigantes occupied a large
area of the north, including Lancashire. In the north-west
it fell to a Gaul, the great soldier and administrator Julius
Agricola, the Provincial Governor, and the XX Legion, to
suppress first the Welsh, then the area that later became
Lancashire, which object he achieved in AD 79. He crossed
into Lancashire via a ford across the Mersey at Latchford.
His strategy was to explore and subdue the estuaries of the
north-west and to send expeditions inland from there to
pacify the hill-dwellers.

The rich agricultural lands of west and south-west
Lancashire were Romanised, but to a significant degree, especially in upland Lancashire, the Romans left the Lancashire

population to get on with life in much the old way, as long as they did not cause trouble. When they did cause trouble, retribution was swift and brutal. Roman civilisation brought few benefits to the remoter areas unless those areas were close to Roman settlements (and significant settlements did grow up around Roman forts such as Ribchester), in which case the local populace was obliged to keep the legions supplied with provisions and services but benefited from this trade, economically.

The Romans were more interested in places further east and north than Lancashire, places where there was military activity and mining to concern them. Lancashire tended to be something of a transit area. That said, the Romans left their mark in terms of towns, forts, camps and roads. The main towns, camps and place-names were as follows:

Bremetennacum (Ribchester)
Coccium (Wigan)
Mamucium (Manchester)
Moricambe Sinus (Morecambe Bay)
Portus Setantiorum (possibly located on the River Wyre in the area of Fleetwood)
Segelocum (Littleborough)

The main Roman roads were:

Chester to Lancaster and Carlisle, via Wigan
Chester to Manchester
Manchester to York
Manchester to Wigan
Manchester to Buxton
Manchester to Ribchester, via Bolton and Blackburn
Ribchester to Ilkley, via the fort at Elslack
Ribchester to Carlisle, via Bowland and the fort at Burrow in Lonsdale (Galacum, Overborough), near Kirkby Lonsdale, the main route to the western end of Hadrian's Wall
Ribchester to Preston and Kirkham, via Longridge
Ribchester to Lancaster, joining Watling Street at Galgate

RIBCHESTER (BREMETENNACUM)

The Roman fort at Ribchester lies on the northern banks of the River Ribble. Indeed, the south-eastern corner of the fort has been washed away by the river. The River Ribble was crossed by a ford close to Ribchester. In the post-Roman era, the Angles acknowledged the presence of the fort by calling it the fort (ceaster) on the Ribble. It was known to be a town of archaeological interest during the reign of Henry VIII, when John Lelland commented around 1540 that: 'Ribchestre …. Hath been an ancient towne. Great squarid stones, voultes and antique coynes be found ther.' Then came William Camden, who wrote an early English travelogue, *Britannia*, in 1586, and who visited Ribchester twice. He recorded the following local rhyme for posterity: 'It is written upon a wall in Rome / Ribchester was as rich as any town in Christendom.' The rhyme seems to reflect a Roman soldier's discharge papers, which refer to a tablet in Rome that recorded the discharge of army units in Ribchester.

The fort was initially built, late in the first century, with a double rampart-and-ditch-system and wooden palisade. These were replaced in the early second century with a stone defensive wall. The size of the fort is 600ft by 440ft. Outside the walls, a fairly extensive civilian settlement (vicus) developed, servicing the garrison. Ribchester was garrisoned by Roman auxiliaries – soldiers from the various Roman provinces – rather than by Romans. Probably the earliest were the Asturian cavalry from northern Spain. After AD 175, Emperor Marcus Aurelius, having defeated the Sarmatians south of the River Danube, in what is now Hungary, levied 5,500 Sarmatian military personnel for service in Britain, many of whom were stationed at Ribchester. Retiring Sarmatian soldiers settled around the fort and no doubt introduced Sarmatian genes into the native Lancastrian population, to add to Spanish genes already present.

In 1796, a boy, playing on the bank of the River Ribble, found, among other things, a fine bronze ceremonial helmet, elaborately decorated and one of the finest examples of its type anywhere in the world. It is housed with the Ribchester hoard in the Romano-British section of the British Museum and is, in my opinion, the finest exhibit in that part of the gallery. It is probably of Asturian origin. There is a tombstone in Ribchester Museum recording the death of an Asturian soldier. Other so-called relics from the Roman fort are the four pillars that support the porch of the White Bull Inn in the village, although it is not certain that these are of Roman origin.

With the conversion of the Emperor Constantine to Christianity in AD 311, the Romans brought Christianity to England and to Lancashire. It is tempting to conclude that this would have affected the lowlanders and those living outside Roman Forts, such as at Ribchester, more than the hill-dwellers, but in any case Christianity died out with the coming of the Angles and Saxons following the withdrawal of the Romans.

THE 'ROMAN' CAMP AT CASTERCLIFFE

Castercliffe, at an elevation of some 900ft, overlooking Nelson and Colne to the north, has long been considered to be of Roman origin. There has been a tendency to call anything antiquated in the area 'Roman'. There are two pack-horse bridges, at Wycoller and Barrowford (Higherford), that have in past times commonly been called 'Roman', but that is not what they are. Castercliffe (also Castelcliffe or Castell Cliffe) itself means 'small fort on a hill'. The site, enclosing over 4 acres, is an oval series of ramparts and ditches, the outer perimeter measuring 350 by 250ft. Two partial sets of ramparts and ditches are recognisable. In the nineteenth century, a third rampart was reported, although this one has disappeared, and the other ramparts were considerably higher than at present. The ramparts are constructed of local stone and earth, and there are post-holes indicating that one or more palisades provided protection. The post-holes contain charcoal, indicating that the pole ends have been partially burned to prevent them rotting in the ground, and there is evidence of burnt oak timbers. There is also the hint of a further palisade outside the outer rampart.

The site has been damaged by the weather, by the pillaging of stone by local inhabitants for the building of walls and farms, and by the ravages of sixteenth-century coal mining since the site represents an outcrop of Coal Measures sitting on Millstone Grit. Records of the halmotte court at Colne (part of the Honour of Clitheroe) dated 1515 include a plea to miners at Castell Cliffe to fill in their disused pits to prevent wayfarers and farm animals from accidentally falling into them.

There is no evidence of human habitation on the site, except for a few flints and Roman coins found nearby. The coins, and the fact that the site stands close to the Roman road from Ribchester to Ilkley, leads to the conclusion that the site is Roman, or at least it might have been temporarily occupied by Romans or their road-building force. However, carbon dating of the charcoal remains dates the site origins firmly in the fourth century BC, or earlier, the timber remains being earlier still. It appears, then, that the fort is of Iron-Age origin, rather than Roman.

THE ROMAN WITHDRAWAL

In the early fifth century, the Romans started to withdraw from Britain. In the first place, attacks from Scottish Picts, Irish Scots and North European Saxons were increasingly difficult to defend. Then there were insurrections within the Empire and invasions of barbarians from without that demanded the concentration of Roman forces overseas. Rome could no longer pay its armies in Britain. In 410, Emperor Honorius is said to have warned that towns would have to look out for themselves. It is conceivable that the occupants of lowland Lancashire and southern England might have said, 'Oh, thank you very much!' in a sarcastic way; the occupants of upland Lancashire might have said the same, but meant it. The Celts had, perhaps, grown soft, shielded by the Romans from their enemies. Romanised Britain, presumably including lowland Lancashire, tried to struggle on as a civilised entity, but the writing was on the wall. Appeals to the Romans, even as late as AD 446, to defend the Celts from the Saxon onslaught fell on deaf ears as the *Pax Romana* (Roman Peace) could no longer be guaranteed and a new era dawned.

THE COMING OF THE ANGLO-SAXONS

Romanised Britain resisted foreign incursions until about AD 450, following which there was a constant flow of Angles into Britain from southern Denmark and Saxons from northern Germany. The Angles attacked the east coast and filtered westwards into Lancashire through the Pennine river valleys, such as the Aire-Calder and Aire-Ribble Gaps. It is not clear whether they drove out the incumbent Celt population or merged with them. No doubt there were some Celts (Britons) who were driven westwards, and their hamlets occupied by Angles, but the population was small, and there was plenty of room for new settlers, so it seems likely that British and Anglian settlements existed in parallel. There was probably interbreeding, forced or otherwise, so it is again likely that Celtic genes survived the onslaught. Anglian place-names are common, but Celtic names survive as well, including Pen in Pendle, meaning hill, and the river name Calder, from *caled* (hard, rocky or rapid), plus *dubro* or *dwr* (water). If the Angles had completely replaced the Celts, there seems little likelihood that they would have retained Celtic place-names, since they would not have been aware of the Celtic names, nor would they have cared about retaining them.

The ownership of the land area which later became Lancashire changed around many times over several centuries, and was sometimes divided at the Ribble. Around AD 500 the Celts won a great victory over the invaders at Mount Badon (Mons Badonicus), the location of which is obscure.

This victory checked the advance of the Angles and Saxons for half a century. In the later sixth century, Lancashire formed part of either Deira, centred on York, or the Celtic kingdom of Strathclyde, stretching down from Scotland. Subsequently, at least part of Lancashire was ruled by the Christian North Welsh. This is the era of the Arthurian legends. In 603, Aethelfrith of Bernicia, King of Anglian Northumbria, whose headquarters was at Bamborough, led a successful military campaign across the Pennines and down the Lune Valley, where he was victorious in battle. Around AD 613, Aethelfrith achieved a much more significant victory, pushing the Welsh back from the Ribble and defeating them at Chester. Lancashire became part of Northumbria, which itself had emerged from a unification of Bernicia and Deira by Aethelfrith, who had married the daughter of Aelle, King of Deira.

Aelle's son, Edwin, challenged Aethelfrith for leadership of Northumbria and Aethelfrith was killed in battle in 616. Edwin, now King of Northumbria, married Aethelburga, Christian daughter of King Aethelbert of Kent. She persuaded him to convert, and he was christened at York in 627. So, after its demise with the withdrawal of the Romans in the fifth century, Christianity once more came to Lancashire and the North.

Edwin was himself killed in battle with Cadwallon, the British (Celt) King of Gwynedd, who was allied with Penda, a growing force in the Saxon kingdom of Mercia, in the Midlands. Penda devastated Northumbria, which was divided once again into its constituent parts of Bernicia and Deira, with Christianity on the wane. Cadwallon also defeated and killed Osric, King of Deira, in 633, but, later that year, the son of Aethelfrith, King Oswald, revered later as St Oswald, had his revenge, defeating and killing Cadwallon at Rowley Burn, south of Hexham. Thus, the kingdoms of Deira and Bernicia were won back and reunited. Lancashire again became part of a Christian Northumbria. Oswald emerged as overlord of all northern and southern England, as the country edged towards unity, but the Saxon heathen

Penda grew in power and defeated and killed Oswald, probably near Oswestry in Shropshire, in 641.

Northumbria divided yet again, with Oswald's brother, Oswiu, becoming King of Bernicia, and Oswine succeeding his father as King of Deira. Oswiu invaded Deira in 651, hoping to unite the kingdoms and causing the death of Oswine, but the ruling classes of Deira had other ideas. Aethelwald, son of Oswald, was chosen to rule Deira under the protection of Penda, who had become leader of the Midlands kingdom of Mercia. Penda hoped to defeat Oswiu, with the assistance of the East Angles and Welsh Britons, but Oswiu won an unexpected victory near Leeds in 654, and, with Penda being killed in the battle, became overlord of most of England. Christian Northumbria effectively extended south to the River Trent, and Lancashire was firmly incorporated within Northumbria for a long period. There is a record of a battle being fought and won by Eardwulf, King of Northumbria, at Billington, near Whalley, in 798.

During the seventh century there had been an accelerated flow of Anglian settlers coming through the Pennine valleys. First, they settled the more fertile valleys and those parts of the southern and western lowlands of Lancashire which were not too swampy to preclude human habitation, possibly reaching the coast. Next, they settled the hill-country. They grew barley and oats and grazed pigs, sheep and cattle on the common lands (heath or woodland). They were, at first, loosely subject to their King, but government gradually developed and they became subject also to the local lord (thegn) and provided labour services or provisions for him in return for his protection. The Angles dominated Lancashire until the coming of the Vikings.

THE VIKINGS

The 'Vikings', the collective name for Norsemen from Norway and Danes from Denmark, came from both the east and the west. From the east, like the Angles before them, the Danes moved across the Pennine valleys during the late ninth century, probably not in significant numbers. They may also have arrived in Lancashire from the direction of the East Midlands-Mercia. In the west, the Norsemen sailed around the north of Scotland (some settling in Scotland) and attacked and settled in Ireland and the Isle of Man in the ninth century. In the early tenth century they settled in the Lancashire river valleys of Wenning, Ribble and Lune, usually occupying slightly higher ground above the flood plains. This was the main period of Viking immigration into Lancashire, and was probably more of a gradual infiltration rather than an invasion. It has been suggested by Walter Bennett that the Viking settlers from the east and those from the west met in the Pendle region, those from the east coast (Danes) reaching Earby and those from the Irish Sea (Norsemen) reaching Whalley.

The chronology of the Viking onslaught is as follows – although it has to be said that Lancashire did not experience the full force of Viking attacks in the way that Northumbria, Yorkshire, Mercia, Wessex and East Anglia did. King Horik of Denmark had imposed discipline on the Danes, not allowing them to raid overseas, but when he died his discipline died with him, and political instability in Denmark encouraged many to turn to overseas raiding. Vikings were attacking the east coast of England as early as the late eighth century, plundering Holy Island in the 790s and attacking the Isle of Sheppey in Kent in 835. The Danes were mainly interested in coastal raiding until the 850s, when they began to extend their visits. In 865 a large Danish army landed, occupied York and made Northumbria subservient to them. They attacked and subdued East Anglia in 869 and moved on to Wessex, reaching Reading in 870. King Aethelred and his brother, Alfred, harried them and inflicted defeat upon them, the first Anglo-Saxon success against the Vikings.

King Aethelred died in 871 and Alfred (the Great) became King, ruling until his death in 899. He was faced with the immediate task of tackling the Danes. His early attempts to hold them were inauspicious. Wessex almost succumbed and Alfred had to pay the Danes, to gain respite. The Danes occupied London in 871 but were obliged to return to Northumbria in 872 to quell a revolt, which they failed to do. They may not have been too interested in the North to persevere, and they returned to the East Midlands to confront Mercia, leaving an Anglo-Saxon, Ricsige, as King of Northumbria, independent of the Vikings and able to reinstate Christianity. Lancashire was presumably included in his kingdom.

In 873, Mercia bought peace with the Danes, leaving Alfred's Wessex to fight on, almost alone. But Alfred had shown that the Danes were not invincible, and, fortunately, in 874 the Danes split their army, half settling in Yorkshire leaving the other half to tackle Wessex in the south. Alfred held his own, the Danes having to be content with settling in the region around, and to the north-east of, Lincoln, Nottingham, Derby and Leicester, but in 878 the Danes again confronted Wessex, advancing to Chippenham, Wiltshire. This is the period of the burnt cakes, when Alfred and Wessex were on the run and close to submission. But, surprisingly, Alfred was able to regroup, and he defeated the Danes, who were forced to sue for peace. Alfred's terms were that the Danish King was to be christened and that the Danes were to leave Wessex. The Danelaw was established, from the East Midlands north-eastwards, where Danish rule prevailed.

Alfred continued to harry the Danes, 886 being a pivotal year when he occupied London and was acknowledged as sovereign of all non-Viking England, but Alfred had no influence in Yorkshire, nor, probably, in Lancashire. Between 892 and 896, another large Danish invading army penetrated from Essex to the Welsh borders. Alfred's son, Edward the Elder, defeated them at Farnham, Hampshire, in 893, but they roamed between Chester, Wales and East Anglia and did not disperse until 896. Viking raids continued until 910, but Alfred's legacy of army reform, fort building, town defences and the creation of a navy kept Anglo-Saxon England in the ascendancy. After Alfred's death in 899, Edward the Elder kept up the pressure, ultimately forcing the Danes to surrender at York.

Meanwhile, King Alfred's daughter, Ethelfleda of Mercia, allowed Norsemen who had been displaced from Dublin in 902 to settle in the Wirral Peninsula and they became established in South Lancashire, where the names Ormskirk, Formby, Crosby and others have Viking origins. Viking names abound elsewhere in Lancashire and the Lake District, with thwaite (a woodland clearing), beck, tarn, gill and fell all being examples. The Lancastrian Norsemen were farmers and became Christian. The Hogs Back tomb at Heysham displays a curious mixture of pagan and Christian designs.

Alfred's son, Edward the Elder (899-934), extended Wessex to the Mersey and built forts at Thelwall, near Warrington, and Manchester. In 924, he was acknowledged as the first King of all England. His son, Athelstan (924-939), drove the Danes out of York. Vikings, aided by Scots and Cumbrians, fought Athelstan at Brunanburh in 937: Athelstan and the Anglo-Saxons triumphed, pushing the border of Anglo-Saxon-controlled England from the Mersey to the Ribble. The location of the Battle of Brunanburh is unknown. It has been suggested that it was fought close to Burnley, with its associations with the River Brun, but this is thought to be unlikely. At this time, both the Danelaw and Anglo-Saxon England was Christian. Lancashire north of the Ribble was in the Diocese of York. Lancashire south of the Ribble was in the Diocese of Lichfield and the whole area was kept as a royal domain.

The Cuerdale Hoard of coins and silver bars, found by workmen on the south bank of the Ribble, between Preston and Blackburn, may have been buried by the Vikings during their retreat from Athelstan in 937, or may alternatively have been associated with the Viking retreat from Edward the Elder in 911. The coins were mostly of Danish origin, minted in York, with some coins of Alfred of Wessex, some of St Edmund of East Anglia, some of Northumbrian kings and some from France.

For much of the tenth century, Alfred the Great's descendants successfully controlled England, including the Danelaw and Northumbria, and including Lancashire. However, in 978 Ethelred II (the Unready) came to the throne, bringing poor government and the installation of favourites in positions of power, alienating much of the nobility and driving them into exile. Viking raids re-commenced in 988 and by 1013 a Danish army had landed. It took control of the Danelaw and Northumbria. Lancashire did not escape the imposition of Danegeld, a crippling tax imposed on the populace to buy off the Danes. Ethelred died in 1016 and was succeeded by Edmund Ironside, who had some successes but did not have full support from his countrymen, and was defeated by the Danes at Ashingdon in 1016. Edmund died in 1017 and Canute, the leader of the Danes, was proclaimed King of all England. The Angle Earl of Northumbria was killed and Canute's brother-in-law, Eric of Hlathir, succeeded him. Lancashire became part of a united, Christian England once again, under Danish rule.

Canute's rule was successful, and, by 1030, Lancashire found itself part of Canute's mini-empire that included the rest of England, Denmark and Norway. Following the death of Canute in 1035, his sons, Harold Harefoot and Harthacnut, ruled for a few years, but the former was murdered and the latter died young, leaving the throne vacant in 1042. Edward the Confessor, son of King Ethelred the Unready and Emma, daughter of Richard, Duke of Normandy, was crowned King. During the weak reign of the Confessor, Earl Godwine, a Wessex Saxon, who had married into the Danish leadership, became the strongest noble in the land. His sons ruled many of the English regions and his daughter married the Confessor. The Confessor died on 5 January 1066, and Earl Godwine's son, Harold, had himself crowned King the following day. He was by no means the only contender, but he seized the hour. It should be noted that both Edward the Confessor and Harold had both Saxon and Viking blood in their veins.

The last fling of the Vikings in the North occurred in September, 1066, just prior to the Norman invasion. King Harold's brother, Tostig, was ruler of Northumbria, including Lancashire north of the Ribble, and was at one time favoured to succeed the Confessor as King. Tostig's rule in the North was harsh and the people rose against him. Harold banished Tostig to Norway, but he returned with King Harald Hardrada of Norway and a Norwegian army. Harold hurried north and defeated Tostig and Hardrada at the Battle of Stamford Bridge, east of York. Meanwhile, William the Conqueror was invading in Sussex and Harold was obliged to make the long journey south to confront him at Hastings.

No doubt the Stamford Bridge encounter, and the associated forced marches, sapped the strength of Harold and his army and rendered them less able to counter the Norman threat. But worse, Harold, seen as an English hero in modern eyes, was not regarded with unswerving adulation at the time and did not carry much of England with him. Indeed, had William not invaded, it is likely that Harold would have faced challenges at home. His army was not strong and was not representative of the whole country. Nor did he have political support overseas. William the Conqueror, on the other hand, had a strong, well-prepared army and had the diplomatic support of the papacy and several European kingdoms. It is to Harold and his army's credit that the Battle of Hastings, fought on 14 October 1066, was by no means a walkover, but ultimately William prevailed. Harold was killed during the battle.

CHAPTER THREE

NORMANS, ANGEVINS, PLANTAGENETS AND WARS OF THE ROSES, 1066-1485

NORMANS, ANGEVINS AND PLANTAGENETS

The Norman Invasion had a greater, more-lasting impact on the social development of Lancashire than any previous invasion. Ironically, Normandy itself had Celtic, Roman, Saxon and Viking origins, much the same as England, William the Conqueror being himself descended from Viking stock. There was, however, no brotherly love felt between William the Conqueror and Harold. William had planned for this day, and, when the opportunity arose, he took it. His reasons were simple. England was a rich land and was in some political turmoil, ripe for the picking. He saw England as richer than Normandy itself, and in any case he intended to keep Normandy under his control as well as subjugating England. His justifications for invading were several. William claimed that he was the rightful heir to the throne of England, given that both he and Edward the Confessor were descended from Richard I of Normandy (as already noted, Emma, daughter of Richard I of Normandy, had married Ethelred the Unready, and the Confessor was their son). Additionally, William claimed that Edward the Confessor had promised to support his claim to succeed Edward. William further claimed that, whilst in Normandy, Harold, too, had sworn that he would support William's claim.

Lord Stanley crowning Henry Tudor at the Battle of Bosworth Field; Richard III died at the head of his army.

The year 1069 saw a revolt in Durham and Yorkshire, with further disaffection in Cheshire, prompting William to carry out his 'harrying of the North', laying waste much of those counties, and probably Amounderness at the same time (although it may be that the damage done to Amounderness had been inflicted during the pre-invasion struggles with Tostig). South Lancashire, the land 'inter Ripam et Mersham' ('between the Ribble and the Mersey'), escaped the devastation as it was a royal estate, but by the time of Domesday Book (1086) Amounderness had still not recovered, with only sixteen of sixty-two manors functioning.

Following the pacification of the North, the Normans imposed their rule. Lancashire had already developed a feudal system under the Anglo-Saxons, as had the rest of the country, the land being divided into manors, each manor ruled by an Anglo-Saxon thegn owing allegiance to the King. Indeed, Edward the Confessor had owned several manors in Lancashire. The Normans strengthened and modified this system. Anglo-Saxon thegns were often replaced by Normans, although the inhospitable nature of the Lancashire landscape meant that there was not the same rush for estates as elsewhere in England. In some cases, the Anglo-Saxon thegns kept their estates, as with Gamel at Rochdale, some having their estates reduced in size.

Under Norman rule, the thegns became lords of the manor, holding their estates from, and owing allegiance to, the King. In return, they had to provide military service to the King, both personally and by raising specified numbers of knights and foot-soldiers to fight the King's wars. The villeins on the manor farmed their own land and kept their own animals, but had to provide services such as haymaking to the lord of the manor. The villeins, bordars and slaves who worked the land were not free, and were not allowed to move from manor to manor. All grain had to be ground at the lord's mill.

At the time of Domesday Book (1086), Lancashire as an entity did not exist, nor did the name 'Lancashire'. Lancashire south of the Ribble was included with Cheshire and those parts of Lancashire north of the Ribble were variously included in Yorkshire, Cumberland and Westmorland. South Lancashire was divided into six 'Hundreds' (administrative units): West Derby (south-west Lancashire); Newton-in-Makerfield (south Lancashire); Warrington (south Lancashire); Salford (south-east Lancashire); Leyland (central Lancashire); and Blackburn (east Lancashire). Newton-in-Makerfield and Warrington were later combined with West Derby. The Hundreds of Amounderness (west Lancashire) and Lonsdale (north Lancashire – 'Lunesdale' – including Furness and the Cartmel Peninsula) were added to south Lancashire to form the old county of Lancashire. Furness and the Cartmel Peninsula were included in Lancashire because the main route into those areas from 'mainland' Lancashire was across the sands of Morecambe Bay, rather than by land across Westmorland or Cumberland.

In 1086, Lancashire was sparsely populated. The original six Hundreds of south Lancashire contained some 180 manors and perhaps were home to just 10,000 people. Much of the land was unsettled and uncultivated moss, heath and woodland. It has been estimated (by Dr. J.J. Bagley) that in the most populous hundred, West Derby, there was as much woodland as arable, and five times more peat-moss than woodland and arable added together. Large tranches of sparsely inhabited heath and open woodland were set aside as 'forests', and reserved for the hunting purposes of the King and his lords, including the forests of Pendle, Trawden, Rossendale, Bleasdale, Quernmore, Fullwood, Myerscough, Over Wyresdale and Toxteth. These areas amounted to perhaps a quarter of the land area of Lancashire.

Under the Normans, Lancashire developed steadily. A few pre-conquest churches, perhaps two dozen, existed, but many more churches were built as the population expanded. Many abbeys and priories were founded, as at Lancaster (the first abbey in Lancashire, founded by Roger de Poitou in 1094), Furness, Conishead, Cartmel, Cockersand, Cockerham, Whalley, Burscough and Penwortham. Burscough Priory was founded by Robert, Lord of Lathom, in 1190. The Cistercian Whalley Abbey was founded around 1300 by Henry de Lacy, transferring from Stanlow in Cheshire, and became a wealthy and powerful establishment. These religious establishments played an important role in caring for the sick, educating the local population, sheltering travellers and providing for the poor. Furness Abbey, founded by Stephen before he became King, provided guides for travellers crossing the sands of Morecambe Bay. A series of motte and bailey castles were built, with wooden buildings standing on earth mounds and surrounded by earthworks, as at Penwortham, Rochdale and Warrington. A few of these were rebuilt in stone at a later date, as at Clitheroe. Town life developed, too, with the granting of rights to hold markets and fairs, and with the emergence of a variety of crafts. King John (1199-1216) developed Liverpool as a staging post for his Irish campaign, and granted the town a charter in 1207. By the end of King John's reign (1216), markets or fairs had been granted at Preston, Warton (in North Lancashire), Lancaster, Liverpool and Warrington, among others, and by the end of Edward I's reign (1307) there were others at Arkholme, Bolton, Burnley, Cartmel, Charnock Richard, Clitheroe, Croston, Dalton-in Furness, Hornby, North Meols (Southport), Ormskirk, Rochdale, Salford, Ulverston, Walton-le-Dale and Wigan. Preston was the first Lancashire town to receive a charter, in 1179. Salford followed in 1230 and Wigan in 1246.

The governance and ownership of Lancashire after the Norman Conquest was dictated by the monarch of the day. William the Conqueror (1066-1087) awarded the lands between the Ribble and the Mersey to Roger de Poitou in return for military services rendered, adding Amounderness at a later date. Roger divided his estates between lesser lords, who owed allegiance to him. One such lesser lord was Roger de Lacy, who held Clitheroe and whose power dominated a large area. Roger de Poitou fell out of favour, and the Conqueror stripped him of most of his estates, but these were restored by the Conqueror's son and successor, William II (also known as William Rufus, 1087-1100), in return for Roger's support. At the onset of the reign of Rufus's brother, Henry I (1100-1135), Roger ruled the whole of Lancashire, including Furness and Cartmel, but he was implicated in a conspiracy against Henry in 1102, was exiled and lost all his estates, which reverted to the Crown.

Henry's nephew, Stephen (1135-1154), held the Honour of Lancaster before he became King. Scottish and Welsh wars troubled Lancashire from time to time during the centuries following the Norman Conquest, and for a time during the reign of Stephen, King David I of Scotland ruled Lancashire, his army having defeated an English force near Clitheroe.

Stephen was followed by Henry I's grandson, King Henry II (1154-1189), who ruled south of the Ribble, with Malcolm of Scotland ruling north of the Ribble, but Henry eventually succeeded in reuniting Lancashire under English control. Lonsdale was incorporated in the county later. Lancashire was first mentioned by that name in documents of 1168-69. Henry's son, King Richard I (the Lionheart, 1189-1199), granted the Honour of Lancaster to his brother, John, in 1189 and appointed the first Sheriff in 1194. John rebelled against Richard, with the support of the Lathom, Molyneux, Montbegon and Boteler families, among others, and, although the rebellion was unsuccessful, the rebels escaped with no greater punishment than fines.

The Lionheart was succeeded by his brother, King John (1199-1216). John de Lacy, Baron of Clitheroe, Roger de Montbegon of Hornby, William Boteler of Warrington and Robert Grelley of Manchester were among the barons who compelled King John to sign Magna Carta at Runnymede in 1215. King John's son, King Henry III (1216-1272), appointed his own second son, Edmund Crouchback, Earl of Lancaster in 1267. Edmund was the founding member of the House of Lancaster but rarely visited Lancashire.

Henry III was succeeded by his son, King Edward I (1272-1307). In 1276, Lancastrians fought in Edward's Welsh campaign, William Boteler of Warrington taking along 200 archers. Boteler also served in Scotland. In 1298, Lancastrians played a part in the defeat of William Wallace at Falkirk. The Model Parliament of Edward I was summoned in 1295, and two representatives from the county and two from the boroughs were called. Liverpool, Preston, Lancaster and Wigan each sent two burghers. The two knights representing the county received 4s recompense per day, the burghers 2s. For much of the thirteenth and fourteenth centuries, no burgesses were sent to Parliament due to the unpopularity of the role and, perhaps, the ravages of plague. Representatives from Lancashire had already attended King John's council in 1213, Simon de Montfort's Parliament in 1265 and subsequent parliaments.

An interesting relic of Lancashire farming from the thirteenth century, or thereabouts, can be found outside the village of Wycoller, near Colne in north-east Lancashire, close to the Yorkshire border. The village boasted two vaccaries, field enclosures for cows or oxen. These vaccaries were bounded, not by hedges or traditional dry-stone walls, but by large vertical slabs of stone (millstone grit) quarried from the nearby moors and erected edge to edge, in a fashion rarely seen in Britain.

Lancashire was in a state of disorder during the reign of Edward I's son, King Edward II (1307-1327); 3,000 Lancastrians were among the English army that fought and was defeated by Robert the Bruce and his Scots at Bannockburn, near Stirling, in 1314. In 1316, the Scots invaded Furness and North Lancashire via the North-east and Yorkshire, and in 1322 the Bruce himself made a foray down the Cumbrian coast, billeting men in Furness Abbey and sacking Furness, Lancaster, Preston and Ribchester, after meeting up with the Earl of Moray (who had already ravaged Lunesdale). The Bruce may have ventured as far south as Chorley. Edward visited Lancashire via Skipton in 1323 to restore order, calling at Blackburn, Wigan, Up Holland and Liverpool. Edward II had been weakened and humiliated by the Scots at Bannockburn and was opposed by his cousin, Thomas, Earl of Lancaster (son of Edmund Crouchback). Thomas had married Alice de Lacy, adding Clitheroe, Penwortham and Widnes to his estates, but she left him in 1317. He was not popular in Lancashire, having employed a hated and unsavoury deputy, Robert Holland, prompting a revolt led by Sir Adam Banastre of Shevington, north-west of Wigan, which was quelled at Deepdale, Preston, in 1315, but only after the rebels had successfully attacked Clitheroe Castle. This revolt caused great disruption on the farms and in the royal forests of Lancashire. Thomas continually challenged Edward II, but was defeated at Boroughbridge, on the River Ure, south-east of Ripon in Yorkshire, in 1322, having been deserted by his henchman, Robert Holland. Thomas was executed without trial in own castle at Pontefract.

Edward II was succeeded by his son, Edward III (1327-1377), during whose reign the Black Death of 1349-51 ravaged Lancashire, killing up to one third of the population. Preston had 3,000 dead, Lancaster 3,000, Amounderness 13,000 and Garstang 2,000. The first Duke of Lancaster was Henry, nephew of Thomas, Earl of Lancaster, and grandson of Edmund Crouchback. Edward III awarded Henry the Dukedom in 1351 in return for his support of the Crown. Henry died in 1361. His daughter, Blanche, married John of Gaunt, son of King Edward III. It was fitting, then, that John of Gaunt was himself appointed Duke of Lancaster in 1377. He was born in Ghent, Flanders, in 1340 (hence his name). Edward III granted him palatinate rights over the county, meaning that Lancashire attained a greater degree of autonomy, compared with other counties, including the right to appoint its own judges. Gaunt was a seasoned military campaigner, overseas, if not an eminently success-ful one, and took Lancastrian soldiers to France and Spain. He built Lancaster Castle, but was an infrequent visitor to Lancashire. He died in 1399.

Edward III was succeeded by his grandson, Richard II (1377-1399), son of the Black Prince. With the death of John of Gaunt, Richard kept the Honour of Lancaster in the hands of the Crown, where it remained in perpetuity (Edward IV formally incorporated the Dukedom into the Crown in 1461). The Dukedom remains vested in the Crown in modern times, so that Her Majesty, Queen Elizabeth II, is also Duke of Lancaster.

THE WARS OF THE ROSES

The Wars of the Roses was not a conflict between Lancashire and Yorkshire. Rather, it was a conflict between the houses of Lancaster and York. The Earls and Dukes of Lancaster rarely visited the county. The Dukedom was not confined to Lancashire, but controlled estates across the country, as the Duchy of Lancaster still does today. No battles were fought in Lancashire, and the protagonists' emblems of red rose and white were not recognised at the commencement of the conflict – the red rose was only adopted as the emblem of the Lancastrian party after the conflict had been underway for some time, while the white rose was not generally adopted as the Yorkist emblem until after the cessation of hostilities. It was, perhaps, during Tudor times that the emblems became firmly recognised as representing the two houses. And it was by no means the case that every one of Lancashire's noble families supported the Lancastrian cause. Harringtons, Talbots and even some Stanleys had Yorkist sympathies. Thomas, Lord Stanley, was Yorkist, but his sons, Thomas (the next Lord Stanley and, later, the 1st Earl Derby) and William were prominent on the Lancastrian side at the Battle of Bosworth Field.

The Stanley family, later to become Earls of Derby (named after West Derby in Lancashire, rather than the East Midlands city of that name), was the most powerful family in Lancashire, and the Stanleys' wealth and importance grew during the Wars of the Roses and the Tudor era, such that they became nationally important, and are well-represented in the following pages.

The first battle of the Wars of the Roses (at St Albans) was not fought until 1455, but the seeds of the conflict were sewn half a century earlier. The conflict was between the Lancastrian camp, being descendents of John of Gaunt (Duke of Lancaster), and the Yorkist camp, being descendants of Lionel (Duke of Clarence) and Edmund (Duke of York). John of Gaunt, Lionel of Clarence and Edmund of York were brothers, sons of King Edward III. The rightful heir to the throne was a fourth brother, Edward, the Black Prince, the oldest son of Edward III, but the Black Prince predeceased his father, and so the succession rested on the son of the Black Prince, Richard II, by-passing the Black Prince's brothers. Richard always suspected that his uncle, Gaunt, coveted his throne, and perhaps with good reason. After all, Gaunt himself had claims to the throne both as a son of Edward III and, through his wife, Blanche, as a descendant of Henry III. Richard also distrusted Gaunt's son, Henry Bolingbroke, an accomplished soldier, who had opposed Richard at one time and tried to change his policies. Richard was not one to forget such slights, and seized the opportunity, when it arose, to banish Bolingbroke into exile for ten years. The seeds of the Wars of the Roses were sown when Richard II again grasped his opportunity, on the death of John of Gaunt in 1399, and divided up the estates of the Dukedom of Lancaster among his friends. To enforce his 'victory' over the Lancastrian line, Richard extended the banishment of Bolingbroke from ten years to life.

Richard II was an unpopular monarch. He favoured his friends, who tended to advise him badly; he ignored the advice of those who knew better, and he showed no magnanimity towards those who opposed him, settling old scores whenever the opportunity arose. He did have one success in defusing the Peasants' Revolt in 1381. The peasants rose in reaction to the poll tax and the general oppression of the masses. Richard was still a boy-King when he bravely rode out to meet Wat Tyler, leader of the Kentish rebels, at Smithfield. The rebels were camped at Blackheath and had already sacked parts of London, gained access to the Tower and executed some of Richard's favourites, but at Smithfield they were courteous towards Richard and he promised them much. According to Lawrence Hill in *Gentlemen of Courage – Forward*, Tyler was arrogant and disrespectful, and may have demanded further concessions from the King, so he was run through with a sword by Ralph Standish, a member of the powerful Lancashire family of that name (and of future *Mayflower* fame). The rebels had already adequately vented their spleen, and they dispersed following the loss of their leader.

Rather foolishly, in 1399, Richard II decided to lead a military expedition to Ireland, leaving his uncle, Edmund, Duke of York, in charge at home. Henry Bolingbroke seized his opportunity and landed at Ravenspur, on the Humber, his aim being ostensibly to recover his Lancastrian estates – but, if things went his way, he intended to seize the throne of his cousin, Richard II. Bolingbroke met up with his Lancastrian retainers and proceeded to Doncaster, where he persuaded the Percys of Northumbria to back him. He then moved on Bath, where the Duke of York, who was ensconced there, surrendered to Bolingbroke without a fight. Bolingbroke progressed to Chester, the seat of Richard's power, and awaited his return from Ireland. Return Richard did, but his troops deserted him and he was captured in North Wales, and taken to London, whose population welcomed Bolingbroke, but eschewed Richard, who had antagonised and alienated them. Richard II was imprisoned in Pontefract Castle and died there, suspiciously, some time later. Henry Bolingbroke had himself crowned King Henry IV.

It may be that a Yorkist (or third party) reaction to the usurpation of Richard's throne would have commenced earlier than it did, if there had been a strong Yorkist contender and if the Lancastrian monarchs had been incompetent rulers, which the first two were not. As it was, Bolingbroke, King Henry IV (1399-1413), did have a troubled reign, not through his own fault, being challenged by the Welsh under Owen Glendower, the Scots, the Percys from Northumberland and the French, putting great strain on his exchequer and damaging his relations with his people, who had to pay for these campaigns. Glendower had great success in Wales, until finally defeated in 1409 by the young Prince Henry (the future Henry V), who Henry IV had appointed Duke of Lancaster. The Percys complained that Bolingbroke had justified his invasion by claiming that he only wanted his Lancastrian estates back, but had then gone further and seized the throne. Henry IV and Prince Henry defeated the Percys at Shrewsbury, in which battle the most famous Percy, Harry Hotspur, was killed.

In return for his support at Shrewsbury, Edward IV appointed Sir John Stanley, of Lathom, to govern the Isle of Man, which remained a Stanley fiefdom for several centuries. Sir John was a minor Cheshire knight who married Isabel, daughter of Sir Thomas Lathom. She was the Lathom heir who brought the estates of Lathom and Knowsley,

Lancashire, into the Stanley family. Sir John made Lathom his home and the wealth and importance of the Stanleys increased steadily. Sir John built Liverpool Tower (demolished in the early nineteenth century and not to be confused with Liverpool Castle) on his estate by the Mersey.

Meanwhile, Henry IV and Prince Henry became estranged as the King's health deteriorated, although formal relations were maintained until the King's death in 1413. Henry V (1413-1422) had a shorter but more glorious reign than his father, with his epic victory over the French at Agincourt in 1415 and elsewhere in France. Sir John Stanley served him well at Agincourt, although he died shortly afterwards, in 1414, and was buried at Burscough Priory. Sir Richard Molyneux of Sefton also served at Agincourt, returning to the country from which his ancestors had departed with William the Conqueror in 1066. Sir Richard Molyneux had an altercation with Sir John's son, Sir Thomas Stanley, in Liverpool in 1424, but the sheriff arrested them both before the two sides, numbering more than 1,000 armed retainers, came into conflict.

Henry V's popularity was high, but his untimely death from dysentery in France left his son, the pious but weak Henry VI, to take over the crown as a nine-months-old boy. Significantly, Henry V's widow, Catherine of Valois, of French royal blood, married Owen Tudor, of Welsh extraction, and initiated the Tudor dynasty, of which more below.

Henry VI (1422-61) was a pious, kind and considerate monarch. For this reason he never lost the love of his people and was regarded by many as a saint after his death. Unfortunately, he was neither a strong ruler nor a warrior-King, and he suffered from mental breakdowns from time to time. Further, he suffered one setback after another in France, losing many of the gains made by his father, Henry V. It has to be said that these French losses could not be wholly blamed on Henry VI. His father had over-extended himself and there was little hope that England could hang on to his extensive French gains indefinitely. Although popular among the masses, Henry VI's weakness and bad government turned the gentry and nobility against him. His challenger, Richard, Duke of York, based his claim on the fact that he was descended on his mother's side from Lionel, Duke of Clarence, and on his father's side from Edmund, Duke of York (to recount, both Lionel and Edmund were sons of King Edward III and brothers of John of Gaunt, great-grandfather of Henry VI. In short, York wanted to rectify the injustice of the usurpation of Richard II's throne by Bolingbroke, Henry IV).

The Wars of the Roses proper began with a minor clash at St Albans in 1455, where Richard, Duke of York, was the victor. Richard did not have public backing to displace Henry, the Yorkists being in a minority throughout the wars, so he established himself as ruler of the kingdom while Henry reigned as titular head. In 1459, the Yorkists defeated the Lancastrians at Blore Heath, near Market Drayton, Shropshire, where Sir William Stanley and Sir Thomas Harrington fought on the Yorkist side. Sir William Stanley was denounced as a traitor by the Lancastrians. His brother, Thomas, Lord Stanley, feigned support for both sides, supported neither and only survived an impeachment attempt by the Lancastrians because Henry VI could not afford to alienate such a powerful family.

The Yorkist success at Blore Heath was reversed at Ludlow and Richard of York had to take refuge in Ireland. He returned after the Yorkists, led by the Earl of Warwick ('the Kingmaker'), had inflicted a bitter defeat on the Lancastrians at Northampton in 1460, gaining custody of Henry VI. Many Lancastrian leaders were killed in this battle and a pattern was emerging of large-scale slaughter, with little quarter given, each party hating the other and seeming to want to annihilate the families of the opposing forces. Richard of York openly claimed the Crown by hereditary right, but the House of Lords refuted his claim, opting for the established order, whilst agreeing that Richard of York should succeed to the throne following the death of Henry VI.

It was not to be. Following the defeat at Northampton, Henry VI was taken to London and installed there again as

titular monarch, but his wife, Margaret of Anjou, a spirited and brave Frenchwoman who played a significant role
in helping Henry to retain the throne, escaped to Wales,
taking refuge with the Tudor family. She had looked after
Henry's interests during his periods of mental breakdown
and she sought to gain support for him in Scotland, Wales
and France. She took with her to Wales their son, Edward,
Prince of Wales, who had been born in 1453. Meanwhile,
a Lancastrian army gathered in the North. Ironically, the
Lancastrians were based in the City of York, and, in 1460,
Richard of York challenged them at Wakefield but was
defeated, losing his life in the process. His son, Edmond,
was murdered whilst escaping. Sir Thomas Harrington and
his son, John, of Hornby Castle, were killed fighting on the
Yorkist side.

At this juncture, the fortunes of the Lancastrian party took
a turn for the worse in that Richard of York's son, Edward, a
skilled military leader, succeeded his father as claimant to the
throne. As Margaret and the Lancastrian army moved south
towards London in 1461, Jasper Tudor, son of Owen Tudor,
brought a Welsh and French force out of Wales to rendez-
vous with them, but was met by Edward, who defeated them
at Mortimer's Cross, near Ludlow. Owen Tudor was captured and was beheaded in Hereford.

Margaret's army continued their march south, pillag-
ing as they went, thereby losing the support of the people
of the south, including, crucially, the support of Londoners.
Before Edward's force returned from Herefordshire, the
Lancastrians defeated Warwick's Yorkist army at Barnet
Heath, near St Albans, and gained custody of Henry VI.
Londoners refused the Lancastrians access to the city, but
subsequently allowed Yorkists Edward and Warwick in.
Edward was declared King, as Edward IV (1461-1483).

Henry VI, Margaret and the Lancastrians returned
north, followed by Edward IV. They fought at Towton,
between Leeds and York, on Palm Sunday in March 1461,
in wintry weather. A snowstorm blowing into the faces of
the Lancastrians greatly impeded them, especially their

archers, and they were forced into the swollen Cock Beck, where many drowned. The Lancastrian cause died with them (for eight years, at least) and the slaughter was great. Edward IV marched through Lancashire and Cheshire to emphasise the magnitude of his victory, and returned to London, leaving Henry VI to rule a mini-kingdom around Bamburgh Castle in Northumberland.

Henry's sojourn in Northumberland ended in 1464 with a skirmish at Hexham, where again the Yorkists were victorious. Margaret and Edward, Prince of Wales, fled to France. Henry was forced to seek clandestine refuge in the North with sympathetic families. He stayed at Appleby (Westmorland), perhaps with the Penningtons at Muncaster Castle, near Ravenglass, in Cumberland, and in Furness. He was the guest of Sir Ralph Pudsay at Bolton Hall, Bolton-by-Bowland, then in Yorkshire, just over the border from Lancashire. He moved to Waddington Hall on the Yorkshire side of the Ribble as secret guest of the Tempests. Tunstalls and Talbots were also sympathetic. How he was betrayed is unclear. It may have been the work of a monk. Jessica Lofthouse has it that a daughter of the Tempests married into the Talbot family and shared her secret with them through her young husband. James Harrington had advised the Talbots of the huge rewards that would result from a betrayal. Henry had wind of the plot and escaped over the Ribble at Brungerley ford (now the site of Brungerley Bridge) but was captured in Clitheroe Wood, perhaps by the Talbots, taken by horse to London, his feet tied to the stirrups, and lodged in the Tower. It might be that the Harringtons intercepted Henry in Clitheroe Wood and were awarded Tunstall estates for their services. John Roby wove his own legend around Henry's sojourn and betrayal in *The Grey Man of the Wood*.

With Henry VI locked away in the Tower, Edward IV reigned on. He married Elizabeth Woodville and thus initiated another struggle, this time between Warwick the Kingmaker and the elevated Woodville family, resulting in much loss of life and Warwick's exile in France. There then followed an unlikely alliance between the Yorkist Warwick and the Lancastrian Margaret aimed at reinstating Henry VI on the throne. The plot was initially successful and Edward IV was forced to take refuge in Holland in 1470. Henry VI was brought from the Tower and duly reinstated, his mother and son remaining in France. But Edward IV returned from Holland in 1471 and on Easter Sunday defeated Warwick at the Battle of Barnet, near St Albans, in which battle Warwick was killed.

At this inopportune moment, Margaret, her son Edward and their followers landed in England and moved towards Lancashire/Cheshire, but tarried a while at Bristol and were intercepted by Edward IV at Tewkesbury. In the battle that followed, Edward IV was victorious and Edward, Prince of Wales, was killed. Margaret surrendered and her husband, Henry VI, was murdered in the Tower by Richard of Gloucester, brother to Edward IV, probably on Edward's orders. There was much bloodletting in and after the Battle of Tewkesbury, leaving the Lancastrian cause defeated for the time being, but Jasper Tudor escaped back to Wales with his nephew, Henry Tudor, the future Henry VII. Henry Tudor was the grandson of Owen Tudor and Catherine of Valois (widow of King Henry V). His parents were Edmund Tudor, Earl of Richmond, and Margaret Beaufort, great-granddaughter of John of Gaunt, Duke of Lancaster, giving Henry his claim to the throne. Margaret Beaufort, incidentally, was a benefactor of Manchester Cathedral, donating the wooden angels that sit high above the nave, playing gilded instruments.

Edward IV reigned successfully, and England prospered during the period of financial stability that he established. He had incorporated the Duchy of Lancaster in the Crown estates in 1461, but as a separate entity to the rest of the Crown lands. He had his brother, George, Duke of Clarence, done away with for treasonable disloyalty (rumoured to have been drowned in a vat of malmsey in the Tower). Edward appointed his loyal brother, Richard of Gloucester (the future Richard III), as steward of the Duchy, and Richard carried out his administrative duties effectively from his castle at Middleham in Wensleydale. Thomas, Lord Stanley, supported the Yorkist Edward in his campaigns in France and was with Richard of Gloucester during his Scottish campaigns, helping to secure Berwick-upon-Tweed for England. But Edward died when only forty years old, in 1483, leaving a twelve-year-old heir, Edward V (1483), a nine-year-old second son, Richard of York, a daughter, Elizabeth of York (later to marry Henry VII) and other daughters.

Richard of Gloucester, brother of Edward IV, seized his opportunity. He was an accomplished administrator and military man, carried out his duties well and was well-esteemed by the people. Thus far he had been loyal to Edward IV, but did not extend that loyalty to Edward's children. On his way south towards London, after the death of Edward IV, Richard overtook Edward's son, Edward V, Prince of Wales, who was being escorted from Ludlow Castle to be enthroned in London. Richard had the most prominent members of the entourage escorted to York, and to ultimate execution at Pontefract. He installed the Prince, of whom he had been appointed guardian, in the royal apartments in the Tower of London, where he was joined by his brother, Richard of York, and the two brothers never re-emerged. Richard had them both murdered and was himself crowned Richard III (1483-1485).

Rumours of the murders became commonplace, as the princes failed to reappear. Public opinion, and opinion in London in particular, turned against Richard. The Stanleys of Lathom and Knowsley remained prominent in matters of state but had to play a cautious role. Thomas, Lord Stanley, was a member of Council but was unhappy with Richard ruling through an inner Council. Lord Stanley was injured when Richard broke up a council meeting at the Tower, but others present suffered worse, Lord Hastings being summarily executed. As the gentry turned against Richard, his closest ally, Lord Buckingham, deserted him and was instrumental in inviting Henry Tudor back from France to displace Richard. A rising in the south, south-west and East Anglia in

1483 was thwarted by bad weather, Henry being prevented from landing. Buckingham was betrayed and executed. The Stanleys avoided being implicated in the Buckingham plot and it may be that their ability to raise a large army of Lancastrians led Richard to overlook their less-than-whole-hearted support – he needed to keep them on his side. He awarded Buckingham lands to Lord Stanley as an inducement to remain loyal. The fact that Lord Stanley, a widower, had married Margaret Beaufort, Duchess of Richmond, who was descended from John of Gaunt and was mother to Henry Tudor of the House of Lancaster, added to Richard's distrust of the Stanleys.

In August 1485, Henry Tudor landed in Milford Haven, Pembrokeshire, meeting up with his uncle, Jasper Tudor, and proceeded up the Welsh coast to North Wales and on to Shrewsbury, unopposed, making contact with the Stanleys and Talbots. Richard III established his military headquarters in Nottingham. His suspicions of the Stanleys were reinforced, Henry Tudor having passed unmolested through Sir William Stanley's territory. Thomas, Lord Stanley, was summoned to Nottingham by the King but sent his son, Lord Strange, in his stead. Richard held Lord Strange as a hostage to ensure Lord Stanley's loyalty, but Strange escaped, and, on recapture, was compelled to reveal that Lord Stanley's brother, Sir William Stanley, was in league with Henry Tudor, despite Richard having favoured him and granted him high office (Chamberlain of North Wales). Richard's suspicions were confirmed.

Henry Tudor met Sir William Stanley at Stafford and Thomas, Lord Stanley, at Atherstone for consultations. The Stanleys could add 3,000 Lancashire and Cheshire men to Henry's army of 5,000, or, alternatively to Richard III's army of 10,000. Richard moved south from Nottingham and the armies met at Bosworth Field, 10 miles west of Leicester. Richard commanded Lord Stanley to join him, otherwise his son, Lord Strange, would be killed – but Lord Stanley refused, declaring that he had other sons! Richard's order to behead Lord Strange was disobeyed by his pragmatic followers, who thought it better to await the outcome of hostilities before taking such precipitate action. Their doubts were reflected throughout Richard's army, many of his reluctant soldiers fighting half-heartedly and some surrendering during the conflict, this being one reason why the conflict only lasted two hours.

The battle of Bosworth Field was fought on 22 August 1485, on a site that turns out to be a mile away from the site traditionally accepted as the battlefield. Sir William Stanley, commanding the Stanley forces that included members of the Standish and Duxbury families from the Chorley district, remained aloof during the early part of the conflict, declining to join Henry Tudor's army but promising to do so when the time was ripe. (I describe this policy as 'tactical lateness', an expression I use to explain my own lateness on occasions!) Despite the Stanleys holding back, and despite Richard's numerical advantage, things were not going well for the monarch, with Northumberland at his rear failing to get involved in the battle. Richard must have realised that his position was perilous. He espied Henry Tudor and his retinue and made a do-or-die attempt to charge and eliminate him, at which point Sir William Stanley and his forces entered the fray, surrounding Richard and killing him. It may be that Sir William himself dispensed the final *coup de grace*. It may also be that Richard's crown, supposedly retrieved from a bush, was placed on Henry Tudor's head by Sir William, or perhaps by Lord Stanley.

Thomas, Lord Stanley, was created Earl of Derby for his crucial support at Bosworth. He died in 1504, aged about seventy, having successfully navigated his way through the quagmire of internecine politics by skilled diplomacy, backing the right side at the right time and remaining neutral at others. He greatly enhanced the Stanley family in terms of land, wealth and power. He left money in his will for the upkeep of the bridges at Warrington and Garstang. His role in Shakespeare plays, especially *Richard III*, is mentioned in the chapters that follow.

CHAPTER FOUR

TUDORS, STUARTS AND THE CIVIL WARS, 1485-1688

THE TUDORS

After Bosworth, Henry Tudor was crowned King Henry VII (1485-1509), initiating the Tudor era. He was descended from Owen Tudor (his grandfather) on his father's side and the Lancastrian John of Gaunt on his mother's side. With his marriage to Elizabeth of York (sister of the murdered Princes in the Tower), he united the Houses of Lancaster and York, effectively bringing to an end the Wars of the Roses.

The final acts in the Wars of the Roses, in so far as the conflict affected Lancashire, were the risings of Lambert Simnel and Perkin Warbeck. Lambert Simnel and his followers, including Sir Thomas Broughton, occupied the castle on the Piel of Fouldray in Morecambe Bay in 1487. Simnel, son of a baker, was the figurehead of the rebellion. It was claimed that he was the Yorkist Earl of Warwick, son of Richard III's brother, the murdered Clarence. His claim to the throne was thin. Henry VII already had the legitimate Earl of Warwick locked away in the Tower, and paraded him through the streets of London to counter Simnel's claim. Simnel sailed from Ireland to the Piel of Fouldray and stayed for several days in the castle. He and his followers then marched through Lancashire to defeat at the battle at Stoke, near

Newark, in Nottinghamshire. Lord Derby's son, George Stanley, Lord Strange, was prominent in this battle, and Henry VII awarded Lord Derby the Furness estates of the defeated Sir Thomas Broughton, together with the Hornby estates of Sir James Harrington and other estates in Salford, as a sign of his gratitude. Perhaps to emphasise his contempt for the rising, Henry VII avoided executing Simnel and magnanimously gave him a job in the royal kitchen!

The Perkin Warbeck affair was more drawn-out and was not so beneficial to the Derbys. Warbeck claimed to be Richard of York, son of Edward IV, one of the Princes in the Tower who was executed on the orders of Richard III. Warbeck was from Tournai, in Belgium, and sailed from Cork to England in 1491, calling himself 'Richard IV'. He was executed in 1499. Sir William Stanley, hero of Bosworth Field and brother to Lord Derby, was implicated in the conspiracy, having apparently made the statement that 'if he were sure that the young man, Perkin Warbeck, was King Edward's son, he would never draw the sword against him.' It may be that Sir William was annoyed that he had not been made Earl of Chester, with palatine powers, and this

Furness Abbey, drawn into these years of conflict.

disgruntlement made him lean towards the impostor. Henry VII had appointed Sir William as Chancellor of the Exchequer and had heaped other honours on him, so that Sir William was said to be the richest man in the realm. Henry may have coveted his estates and had him executed in 1495, the most-prominent victim of the Perkin Warbeck affair, at which point his estates reverted to the Crown. Unusually, Henry paid for Sir William's funeral – he could afford to, given the wealth that he had gained from Sir William's death!

Thomas Stanley, Lord Derby does not seem to have been unduly troubled by the execution of his brother, Sir William. On the contrary, it seems that Henry VII was more regretful of his actions than Lord Derby. He visited Lord Derby at Lathom, perhaps to make atonement or to emphasise that he had no argument with Lord Derby. There is a tradition that Henry was escorted to the roof area, to survey the surrounding estates, and that Lord Derby's fool saw an opportunity for Lord Derby to take his revenge on the King for the execution of Sir William. It seems that, as the King looked down from his unprotected perch, the fool whispered to Lord Derby: 'Tom, remember Will'. Lord Derby did not respond to the prompting, and the King sensed the tension and retreated downstairs, briskly. Incidentally, in preparation for Henry's visit to Lathom, Lord Derby funded the building, or perhaps the repair or rebuilding, of the bridge over the Mersey at Warrington, which Henry crossed on his perambulation from Lathom to Manchester. As for Henry, it has been claimed that, he was so impressed with Lathom House that he had Richmond Palace restored in a similar style ('like Lathom Hall in fashion').

Henry VII had a daughter, Margaret, sister to Henry VIII. Margaret married King James IV of Scotland, thereby initiating the dynasty which included Mary Queen of Scots and James VI of Scotland/James I of England. Sir Edward Stanley, the fifth son of Thomas, Lord Derby, escorted Margaret to Scotland in 1503 for her wedding. He was a cultivated individual, and played the clavichord and sang for the royal pair, much to their enjoyment. Sir Edward's next meeting with James IV, at the battle of Flodden in 1513, was not so convivial. Sir Edward was not only skilled in the arts. He was an accomplished military man. Following the death of Henry VII in 1509, his son Henry VIII (1509-1547) had been crowned King. Whilst Henry VIII was in France, sparring with the French, his brother-in-law James IV of Scotland seized the opportunity to aid the French and to further the interests of Scotland by invading England. An English army was raised in the North, including the same Sir Edward Stanley, plus Sir William Molyneux of Sefton, Sir Henry Norris of Speke and Sir Richard Assheton of Middleton. With a strong Lancastrian contingent, the English army met the Scots at Flodden in 1513. The Lancastrian archers did great damage. Sir Edward Stanley and his men were instrumental in defeating the Scots, whose King, James IV, lost his life in the mayhem. Sir Edward was created Lord Monteagle for his services, and was said to have built the chapel at Hornby Castle in thanksgiving. A memorial window in Middleton Church and brasses in Sefton and Childwall Churches record the victory at Flodden, as does the Regimental Chapel built by the Stanleys in Manchester Cathedral. Sir Walter Scott in his *Marmion* recorded the exploits of the Lancastrians:

> Let Stanley charge with spur and fire,
> With Chester charge and Lancashire.

Another ballad of the time recorded that:

> From Warton unto Warrington,
> From Wigan unto Wyresdale,
> From Weddecon [Wedacre, near Garstang] to
> Waddington,
> From Ribchester to Rochdale,
> From Poulton to Preston, with pikes,
> They with Stanley out went forth.
> From Pemberton and Pilling dikes,
> For battle billmen bold were bent.

Sir Edward Stanley, Lord Monteagle, had gained possession of Hornby Castle, near Lancaster, through his marriage to the daughter of Sir John Harrington, of Hornby Castle. Sir John had been killed at Wakefield, with his father, during the Wars of the Roses, and his two daughters became wards of Lord Stanley, so it seemed pragmatic for one of the daughters to marry Lord Stanley's son, Sir Edward. Suspicions were raised when a cousin of Sir Edward's wife died, possibly due to poisoning, and Sir Edward was able to add the cousin's estate to those he already owned. Much has also been made of Sir Edward's alleged atheism and involvement in sorcery, as recounted by John Roby in his *Traditions of Lancashire*. He is said to have considered life to be like wound-up clock-work – once wound down there was nothing left.

Sir Edward's military ability was admired and valued by Henry VIII, who ennobled him, as Lord Monteagle, at Eltham Palace, Kent (now south-east London), in 1514. Henry would greet Sir Edward with the words, 'Ho! My soldier!' The greeting, 'Yo, Blair!' bestowed on Prime Minister Tony Blair by President George W. Bush in modern times is, perhaps, reminiscent of Henry's greeting to Lord Monteagle! Sir Edward went to France with Henry VIII and was present at the Field of the Cloth of Gold in 1520, but died in 1523.

Sir Edward Stanley's eldest brother, George, predeceased their father, and so it was George's son, another Thomas, who became the second Earl of Derby in 1504 on the death of his grandfather, Thomas, the 1st Earl. George had married the heiress to the Strange family title and their son, another Edward, became Lord Strange. At the tender age of eleven, or so, Edward, Lord Strange, inherited the Earldom of Derby as 3rd Earl. He was tutored by Cardinal Wolsey and became a faithful servant of Henry VIII and 'Cupbearer' to Anne Boleyn. He was one of the nobles who communicated Henry's decision to divorce Catherine of Aragon to Pope Clement VII. Edward supervised the Dissolution of the Monasteries in Lancashire and was instrumental in putting down the northern insurrection known as the Pilgrimage of Grace in 1536. The Dissolutions in Lancashire had started in 1536 with the demise of Burscough, Up Holland and Cartmel Priories, these three falling within the first category of those to be dissolved, having a value of less than £200 per annum.

The Pilgrimage of Grace, led by Robert Aske, a Yorkshire-man, was a reaction to discontent arising from a variety of causes, including Henry's Dissolution of the Monasteries, his split with Rome, the raising of taxes, agricultural enclosures and higher rents and prices. One aspect of the movement was enlightened – a demand for a freely-elected Parliament, in York. The rebellion was aimed at Henry's Vicar General, Thomas Cromwell, rather than the King, since Cromwell was considered to be the source of all these evils, and the reformed Parliament was intended to curb the powers of such high officials. The Abbots of Furness and Whalley Abbeys were drawn into the uprising, possibly against their better judgement, and on the failure of the enterprise they paid the price. Abbot John Paslew of Whalley Abbey was hanged at Lancaster and his abbey dissolved in 1537. John Roby wrote a dramatised version of this story in 1829 and Harrison Ainsworth's *The Lancashire Witches* (1848) contains another version. The Abbot of Furness and his Abbey suffered a fate similar to Abbott Paslew and Whalley Abbey. Edward, third Lord Derby, implemented Henry's policy of promising much to the rebels, causing them to withdraw from the rising, and then arresting the leaders of the revolt. He also participated in Henry's war with Scotland in 1542.

Henry's reign initiated the Reformation, a religious upheaval that was a feature of Lancashire life through two centuries, centuries characterised by the persecution of Catholics and Nonconformists (and, in Mary's reign, Protestants), priest-holes, recusancy (where failure to attend reformed church services resulted in fines and imprisonment), and occasional conflicts where opposing forces were divided along religious lines. Prior to 1541, the ecclesiastical government of Lancashire was divided between York and Lichfield, but in that year Lancashire was united ecclesiastically under the governance of Chester.

Henry VIII was succeeded by his son, Edward VI (1547-1553), whose short reign was followed by the even shorter reign of his half-sister, Mary (1553-1558). Edward, Lord Derby, must have impressed Mary as he was soon appointed to important positions within her government. He participated in the trial of Lady Jane Grey, great-niece to Henry VIII and a potential challenger for Mary's throne. Lady Jane was executed in 1554. Queen Mary attempted to reverse the religious changes brought about by her father, causing the persecution of Protestants such as John Bradford, of Manchester, who was burned at the stake in Smithfield, London, and George Marsh, Vicar of Deane. Surprisingly, Edward, the 3rd Earl of Derby, having served Henry VIII in imposing the Reformation on Lancashire, now changed his religious spots, assisting Mary in her reactionary policies. Edward was, for instance, involved in the trials of George Marsh, leading to his execution in 1555.

During the reign of Queen Elizabeth I (1558-1603), Edward once again changed his spots and assisted in the implementation of Elizabeth's Protestant policies. In 1569, there occurred the Rising in the North, an attempt to replace Elizabeth on the throne with the Catholic, Mary Queen of Scots. This uprising did not particularly involve Lancashire, although Sir John Southworth of Samlesbury was involved and was lucky to avoid execution. The rising was defeated, and 800 executions followed.

One of the features of Elizabeth's reign was the threat from Spain. The Armada was defeated in 1588, and fears of a Spanish landing in Lancashire led to the renovation of Lancaster Castle and the castle on the Piel of Fouldrey in Morecambe Bay. Elizabeth was popular in Lancashire, even among Catholics and Nonconformists, the growth of national feeling under the threat of foreign dominance blurring religious divisions. However, persecution of 'massing Catholics' continued, and the Catholic gentry, such as the Norris family of Speke Hall, continued to play an important role in harbouring Catholic priests. At Speke Hall, on the banks of the Mersey Estuary, south-east of Liverpool, a spy-hole over the main entrance, with space for a hidden observer under the eaves to spy on visitors to determine their friendliness or otherwise, is of a type that gives rise to the expression 'to eavesdrop'.

Edward, the 3rd Earl, died in 1572, and his son, Henry Stanley, 4th Earl of Derby, was equally faithful to Elizabeth in committing papists for trial at Chester Castle. Henry was Lord Lieutenant of Lancashire and Cheshire, and Lord of Man, the latter title being virtually hereditary within the Stanley family. Henry had already made a name for himself during Mary's reign, marrying Lady Margaret Clifford, a descendent of King Henry VII. Queen Mary and Phillip of Spain were present at the wedding ceremony, indicating the importance of the occasion. Henry served Elizabeth well and was an official at the trial of Mary Queen of Scots, who was executed in 1587.

It has been estimated that Lancashire in the mid-sixteenth century was home to less than 100,000 people. As a gauge of its lack of economic importance, nationally, Lancashire in 1504 was responsible for providing less than 1 per cent of the grant made by Parliament to Henry VII. However, things were stirring, and Lancashire was benefiting from the Tudor prosperity initiated by Henry VII, following the long years of political upheaval during the Wars of the Roses. The most important town was Manchester, already the main centre for textile merchants to ply their trade. The other main towns were Preston, Lancaster and Wigan. Woollen textiles predominated (wool weft with flax warp), although fustians (cotton weft with flax warp) made an appearance. Cotton was introduced into England by the East India Co., but its use was greatly limited by regulations presumably designed to protect the woollen industry. In 1540, Leland, on his travels, noted that a certain Mr Bradshaw of Wigan had found canel, or sea-coal, on his land and was exploiting it, as were others in Bolton-le-Moors. These coal and textile developments were signs of things to come. The enclosure movement was underway, leaving less land for agriculture and more for animal husbandry, especially the rearing of sheep and cattle.

It was little wonder that farmers and farm workers looked to textiles to supplement their meagre incomes.

Henry Stanley, 4th Earl of Derby, died in 1593. He was succeeded as 5th Earl of Derby by his son, Ferdinando Stanley, Lord Strange, who married a Spencer of Althorpe in Northamptonshire. As noted elsewhere, Ferdinando had a keen interest in the theatre and was acquainted with William Shakespeare, sponsoring a group of actors that performed Shakespeare's works, among others. Through his mother, Margaret Clifford, Ferdinando was descended from King Henry VII (Henry was his great-great-grandfather), and, with Queen Elizabeth failing to provide or nominate a successor, Ferdinando was touted as a possible candidate, a proposition that initially might have appealed to him, although it has been suggested that he was alarmed at the dangerous prospect and rejected it immediately. Elizabeth tended to deal harshly with prospective rivals and aspirant successors. Her spies learned of the plot and Ferdinando, it seems, quickly lost his enthusiasm for the escapade, if he ever had any. He betrayed fellow-plotter Sir Richard Hesketh of Rufford, who was executed for his role in the affair. Ferdinando survived, but died shortly afterwards, probably from poisoning, having been 5th Earl for only six months. He may have been poisoned in retribution for the betrayal of Hesketh. Ferdinando was succeeded by his brother, William, who was 6th Earl of Derby during the later years of Elizabeth's reign and throughout the reign of James I, dying in 1642. It has been postulated that William, among others, was the true author of some of Shakespeare's plays, and Shakespeare has other connections with Lancashire, as detailed below.

SHAKESPEARE AND LANCASHIRE

It may be that William Shakespeare visited Lancashire with the Queen's Players in 1589. According to the Stanley Papers issued by the Chetham Society, the Derby Household

Book records the visits of the Queen's Players to New Park, Lathom, in 1588 and to Knowsley in 1590, New Park and Knowsley being the Lancashire houses of the Stanley family, the Earls of Derby. A letter from Baron Scrope dated September 1589 (see below) is further evidence of the Queen's Players visit to Lancashire. It is tempting to assume that Shakespeare accompanied them.

If Shakespeare was with the Queen's Players on these occasions, then these may not be his first visits to Lancashire, nor, indeed, his first visits to Lathom. There is a tradition (supported by some evidence) that Shakespeare lived in Lancashire as a teenager, during his 'missing years'. He may have needed to escape from Stratford-upon-Avon for some delinquency, such as poaching deer. It would appear that he became tutor to the children of the Hoghton family of Hoghton Tower, between Preston and Blackburn, fulfilling a second role as a player. Anthony Holden (William Shakespeare, *His Life and Works*) suggests that Shakespeare, when not quite fifteen years old, joined Lord Strange's Men when they visited Stratford in 1579 and travelled to Lancashire with them, possibly with a letter of commendation from his Stratford schoolmaster, John Cottom, to Alexander Hoghton of Lea (Lord Strange was Ferdinando Stanley, of Lathom, later 5th Earl of Derby). In his will, Alexander Houghton makes a bequest to his half-brother, Thomas, as follows:

> It is my mind and will that the said Thomas Hoghton my brother shall have all my instruments belonging to musics and all manner of play clothes if he be minded to keep and do keep players. And if he will not keep and maintain players, then it is my mind that Sir Thomas Hesketh knight shall have the same instruments and play clothes. And I most heartedly require the said Sir Thomas to be friendly into Fulk Guillom and William Shakeshafte now dwelling with me and either to take them into his service or else help them to some good master as my trust is he will.

This will is dated 1581. Shakespeare was seventeen years old. It is not unusual for variations of a name to be used, and 'Shakeshafte' was a not-unusual version of his name. As a 'player', Shakespeare would tutor the family's children during the day and play music and perform in plays in the evening to entertain the family and guests.

The Hoghton and Hesketh families were Catholic, as was Shakespeare's family, in times when Catholic priests were regularly executed and non-attendance at reformed churches by Catholics (recusancy) was punished with stiff fines. Shakespeare may have been Oxford University material, and his school regularly sent students to Oxford, but he may have been unable to swear the oaths of loyalty that were a prerequisite to attendance, so Oxford was denied him.

It has been proposed by Helen Moorwood that Shakespeare's father, John Shakespeare, was of Lancashire origin, possibly from Preston, in which case he would have had family connections in Lancashire. Helen Moorwood also suggests that Mary Arden was John Shakespeare's third wife, and not William Shakespeare's mother as is traditionally accepted. William's mother was John's second wife, and is of unknown origin. It is tempting to think that, if this is true, then William Shakespeare's mother, as well as his father, may have been Lancastrian.

Another person mentioned in Alexander Hoghton's will was John Cotham (Cottom), a Catholic, who was a master at Shakespeare's school in Stratford, and who was also Lancastrian, with a wide range of Catholic contacts in Lancashire. As mentioned above, he may have arranged to take Shakespeare to Lancashire and place him with a Catholic family of his acquaintance, the Hoghtons.

Shakespeare stayed with the Hoghtons for up to two years, then in 1581 moved on to Rufford Hall to serve the Hesketh family. Not far from Rufford Hall is New Park, the house at Lathom belonging to the Stanley family, the first family of Lancashire. The Stanleys and the Heskeths were close, both geographically and in terms of social contact. It is apparent that William Shakespeare moved rapidly on from the Heskeths at Rufford to the Stanleys. The head of the Stanley family was Henry, the 4th Earl of Derby, whose son, Lord Strange, ran a group of players, Strange's Men. This was Shakespeare's big chance and he joined the group and benefited from the Derby's social status in London, becoming a member of a top group of actors there.

Whether or not Shakespeare ever visited Lancashire, certain Lancastrians, namely the Stanleys/Derbys, had a role to play in Shakespeare's works. During the fifteenth century, the Stanleys of Lathom and Knowsley were the most important family in Lancashire and played an important role in English history. For this reason alone it is not surprising that William Shakespeare included them in his history plays, *Henry VI* (Parts 2 and 3) and *Richard III*, written between 1587 and 1592. But there were other reasons for their inclusion. Firstly, in relating these histories, written as they were a century or more after the events depicted in them, Shakespeare recognised the continuing importance of the Stanleys/Derbys in national affairs. Indeed, as related elsewhere in this book, Ferdinando (Lord Strange, who, as already noted, became the 5th Earl of Derby in 1593, albeit briefly) was great-great grandson to King Henry VII, and was mentioned as a possible successor to the childless Queen Elizabeth. Shakespeare's inclusion of the Stanleys in his histories pays homage to them as a continuing powerful force in the country. Secondly, Shakespeare probably performed for the Stanleys/Derbys in Lathom or Knowsley, or both, in his younger days and benefited from their hospitality. As mentioned above, he may have travelled to Lancashire with Lord Strange's Men as a youth and he continued to have links with the theatrically-inclined Ferdinando. It would not be surprising if Shakespeare's links with the Stanleys/Derbys led to him developing ties of loyalty towards them.

THE FIRST STUART – JAMES I

When Elizabeth died in 1603, she was succeeded by James VI of Scotland, who became King James I of England (1603-1625). James VI became known as 'the wisest fool in Christendom' and 'our English Solomon' as a result of some of the dubious decisions he made in governing the country. He was the son of Mary Queen of Scots and the great-grand-son of Margaret, sister to Henry VIII. It may be remembered that Margaret had been escorted to Scotland for her wedding in 1503 by Sir Edward Stanley, later to become Lord Monteagle.

In August 1617 James paid a royal visit to Lancashire. He processed from Carlisle to Hornby Castle, home of Lord Monteagle, then to Ashton Hall, Lancaster, home to Lord Gerrard. He next visited Myerscough Lodge, where he hunted, and from where, on 15 August, he ventured into Preston for a civic banquet at the Guildhall. He arrived at Hoghton Tower, home to the Catholic de Hoghton family, on the 16th and spent three days there. The Tower, located on the road from Preston to Blackburn, was built in 1565 by Thomas Hoghton. James' visit reduced the head of the family, Sir Richard Hoghton, to penury, resulting in several years' incarceration in the Fleet debtors' prison in London (the temporary abode of Dickens' Mr Pickwick, two centuries later). Another member of the Lancashire gentry at Bartle Hall, near Preston, burned his house down rather than have the monarch visit him, fire being the cheaper option. Whilst at Hoghton Tower, James visited Sir Richard's local alum mine, was entertained by masques and rush-bearing ceremonies and famously, if only in legend, knighted the loin of beef, rendering it sirloin. Harrison Ainsworth paints a vivid picture of the goings-on at Hoghton Tower in *The Lancashire Witches*. After Hoghton Tower, James visited the Derby family at Lathom and finally Bewsey Hall, near Warrington, home of Thomas Ireland.

Whilst in Lancashire, and probably while he was at Myerscough Lodge, James received a petition from his

Lancashire subjects, urging him to relax the puritanical ban on many sports being practiced on Sundays. He received the petition sympathetically, and the populace had their request granted, although some sports, such as bear-baiting and football, remained banned. The new guidelines were contained within the *Book of Sports*, published in 1618.

James I brought with him from Scotland a prejudice against witches and witchcraft. Whilst still King of Scotland, James decided to marry Anne of Denmark, daughter of the King of Denmark, and in 1589, Ann duly set sail from Denmark but sailed into a heavy storm. Her mistress of the robes, Jane Kennedy, was washed overboard and drowned, and the ship was blown off course and landed in Norway. The impetuous James sailed to Norway and married Ann there. Two Scottish women were accused of raising the storm that threatened Anne, and were duly tried for witchcraft, convicted and burnt at the stake. If James VI was not keenly anti-witch before that time, he certainly was afterwards. In 1597, James' book *Daemonologie* was published, 'Daemonologie' being the short version of the long Latin title. In his book, James expounded his thoughts on witchcraft and the book became the blueprint for lawyers and law-enforcers interested in prosecuting witches. *Daemonologie* was important in establishing the thoughts of the monarch throughout the realm. This was especially so when James VI of Scotland came south and became James I of England. It legitimised an activity – witch-hunting – that became something of a fashion. Justices of the Peace, lawyers and any of the gentry of the land who wanted to attract the attention of the King could perhaps do so by prosecuting witches.

The Pendle Witches paid the price of King James' prejudice, combined with the superstitious nature of the population at the time and the self-condemnatory acts of the witches. They lived in and around Pendle Forest, an area of north-east Lancashire, dominated by Pendle Hill and surrounded by the towns of Burnley, Colne, Whalley and Clitheroe. Most of the witches were beggars, some young, some old, who, if they had a business plan, would include in it the suggestion that, if you were going to beg, your turnover would likely increase if your customers were afraid of you. And afraid of witches their customers were, at least in some part. No doubt the witches were malignant, not nice people, who in some cases really believed in their own supernatural powers. Certainly some of the local population believed in those powers. Illness and death among people and livestock were common happenings, as were crop failures and other natural events, for which witchcraft provided a believable explanation.

The witches were prosecuted in 1612 by Roger Nowell, a Justice of the Peace, of Read Hall, near Padiham. I dare say that the main topic of gossip between my own Duxbury ancestors and their neighbours around 1612 was the local upsurge in witchcraft – they lived in the Altham area, just a mile from Read Hall and just a few miles from the witches themselves. Nine of the accused were tried at Lancaster Castle, found guilty and hanged. A tenth accused, the frail and elderly Elizabeth Southerns, alias Old Demdike, had died in the cells before being brought to court. 'Witch' Alice Nutter, of Roughlee Hall, near Nelson, was the relatively wealthy widow of a yeoman and was the only one of the accused to refuse to confess. She may well have been innocent and may have been framed.

Such was the interest in witches, countrywide, that they even found their way into English literature. A letter dated 1589 from Baron Scrope, of Bolton Castle, Wensleydale, Yorkshire, Governor of Carlisle, to William Asheby, English ambassador at the court of King James VI in Edinburgh, reads as follows:

After my very hartie comendacions: upon a letter receyved from Mr Roger Asheton, signifying unto me that it was the kinge's ernest desire for to have her Majesties players for to repayer into Scotland to his grace; I dyd forthwith dispatche a servant of my owen unto them wheir they were in the furthest parte of Langkeshire, whereupon they made their returne heather to Carliell, wher they are, and have stayed for the space of ten dayes, whereof I thought good to gyve yow notice in respect of the great desyre that the kyng had to have the same to come unto his grace; And withal to praye yow to gyve knowledge thereof to his Majestie. So for the present, I bydd yow right hartelie farewell. Carlisle the xxth September, 1589. Your verie assured loving frend, H. SCROPE.'

In this letter, Henry Scrope tells William Asheby that King James VI has asked for the Queen's Players (Queen Elizabeth's players, that is) to go to Scotland. Scrope says that he had located the players in Lancashire and that they had returned to Carlisle. They presumably journeyed on from there to Edinburgh to play for the King.

It has been conjectured that William Shakespeare was among the Queen's Players, and journeyed with them through Lancashire and then via Carlisle to Edinburgh. The date of the letter, 1589, is the year that James' wife, Anne of Denmark, had problems with the storm, whilst sailing to Scotland. It has further been conjectured that Shakespeare may have been in Edinburgh at the time of the witch trial there, but in any case at least he would have known about the trial, and the fate of the Scottish witches. It is no coincidence that the most famous witches in English literature are the witches in *Macbeth*, Scottish witches in a Scottish play written by William Shakespeare around 1606. It is no coincidence, either, that the play makes reference to storms at sea in two places: referring to a sailor, one witch says that 'Though his bark cannot be lost, Yet it shall be tempest-tost;' and in describing the mischief that the witches get up to, *Macbeth* refers to 'the yesty waves' that 'Confound and swallow navigation up', no doubt harking back to the near drowning of Anne of Denmark. By including witches in *Macbeth*, Shakespeare was pampering to King James's prejudice against witches, whilst also reflecting and reinforcing popular opinion of the times.

A further outbreak of witchcraft occurred in 1633, when eleven-year-old Edmund Robinson, of Wheatley Lane, near

Nelson, claimed to have witnessed a witches' coven and was escorted by his father around local churches, identifying women who he claimed to have been present at the coven. Nineteen women were tried at Lancaster and found guilty of witchcraft. However, these were more-enlightened times. Charles I was on the throne, and, on hearing of the trials, he summoned four of the witches to London, where they were examined by 'experts', including William Harvey (the same William Harvey who first discovered the circulation of blood in the human body). Charles himself participated in the examinations. Nothing incriminating was found and the order given to release all the convicted women.

THE LATER STUARTS AND THE CIVIL WARS

James I died in 1625 and was succeeded by his son, Charles I (1625-1649). If the Wars of the Roses saw no significant battles in Lancashire, the Civil Wars period, followed by the Jacobite risings, certainly made up for it. Had Charles been an able administrator he might have avoided civil war. Had he been an accomplished military leader he might have defeated the Parliamentarians. As it was, he was neither of these. He was autocratic, with his Court of Star Chamber dispensing arbitrary justice. He raised too many taxes, including the notorious ship money tax for the Navy; he claimed ancient lapsed feudal rights to increase his income and he demanded men for the Scottish war of 1638, including 750 from Lancashire. He was more unpopular among certain sections of the populace than among others. Puritans had become a strong section of society and were anti-monarch because of Charles' Catholic leanings, his persecution of Puritans, and the royal acceptance of the right of the populace to enjoy sports on Sundays. Charles was at odds with his Parliament. He claimed the divine right of kings to govern without hindrance, and reigned without Parliament for eleven years. Parliament did not accept his divine right to rule, and rebelled against him.

As elsewhere, the farmers and gentry of Lancashire were disgruntled, leading them to petition Parliament against the corrupt election of knights in 1640. Lancashire tended to be Puritan in the south-east and Catholic in the north and west. The county was fairly equally divided between Royalists and Parliamentarians, as indicated in its representation in the Long Parliament, with eight Parliamentarians and six Royalists (or possibly seven of each). Lancashire had been prosperous prior to the Civil Wars, but was brought low by a combination of war, hunger and recurring plague. Plague ravaged Manchester in 1605 and 1645, Liverpool in 1644-45, Ormskirk in 1647, Warrington in 1650 and Preston, which lost over 1,000 of its inhabitants, one-third of the total population of the town, in 1631,

In 1641, Parliament took charge of the army and the Royalist Lord Strange (soon to be the 7th Earl of Derby) was replaced by the Parliamentarian Lord Wharton as Lord Lieutenant of Lancashire, responsible for raising local contingents for the national army. Royalist magistrates were removed and Parliamentarian MPs Ralph Assheton, Richard Shuttleworth, Alexander Rigby and John Moore were sent to Lancashire to review military preparedness.

Royalist James Stanley, Lord Strange, 7th Earl of Derby, succeeded to the latter title in 1642. His wife, the Countess of Derby, was Charlotte de Tremouille, of French nobility. Initially, they were gay courtiers, friends of Prince, later King, Charles and his wife Henrietta Maria. Lord Strange fought in Scotland for Charles I in 1638-39. As during the Wars of the Roses, the Derbys were the strongest and most important family in Lancashire, and south-west Lancashire followed them in support of the King. Lord Strange was present at a gathering of 5,000 citizens at Fulwood Manor, near Preston, on 20 June 1642, the meeting having been called by the Royalist High Sheriff of Lancashire, Sir John Girlington, ostensibly to read out decrees received from the King and to hear the King's reply to the Lancashire petition. The assembly moved on to Preston Moor and developed into a demonstration along party lines, 400 declaring for the King and most of the remainder calling for a King-and-Parliament reconciliation.

There was to be no reconciliation. Parliamentarian Manchester became alarmed at the Royalist stance and took up arms for the defence of the town. Either provocatively or misguidedly, Lord Strange and Sir Thomas Tyldesley met for dinner and consultations in Alexander Green's house in Manchester on 15 July 1642. Their presence was discovered by the Parliamentarians, and a skirmish ensued, during which the Royalists were obliged to retreat. Richard Percival, a Levenshulme weaver and a Parliamentarian, was shot in the skirmish, the first person to die in the Civil War in Lancashire, possibly the first to die in England. In the same month, Sir John Girlington seized the Preston armoury for the Royalists and Lord Strange did the same in Liverpool. Lord Strange was sacked as Lord Lieutenant of Chester and North Wales for raising Royalist recruits in Lancashire.

Later in 1642, Lord Strange and Sir Gilbert Gerrard, Lord Molyneux, Sir John Girlington, Lord Rivers and an army of 4,000 tried to take Manchester but were unsuccessful, losing 200 men, compared with just half a dozen Parliamentarians deaths. Thomas Standish of Duxbury, leader of the Leyland Royalists, was killed by a musket shot from the church steeple. The Standishes of Standish were Royalist, but the Standishes of Duxbury were mostly Parliamentarian, Thomas being an exception. A professional German soldier, Colonel Rosworm, had been hired to organize the defences of Manchester, assisted by Captain Bradshaw and Captain Radcliffe. (It appears that Rosworm might have fought on the Royalist side if a timely offer had been made to him, Lord Derby having invited him to Lathom, but he opted to honour his agreement with Manchester, 'honesty being more worth than gold'.) Barricades and other obstacles were erected at strategic points to prevent a Royalist incursion and the inhabitants of Manchester supported the defenders effectively. The Royalists camped in Sir Edward Mosley's estate (the 'Lodge') and bombarded Deansgate from Salford, with little effect. Unable to breach the town defences, the Royalists offered to withdraw from the town in return for a payment of £1,000 plus the armaments in the possession of the defenders. The Parliamentarians rejected the offer, which prompted the Royalists to offer withdrawal in return for just a part of the defenders' armaments, an offer that was also rejected.

Lord Strange became the 7th Earl of Derby during the siege, his father having passed away, and on 30 September 1642 the new Lord Derby was ordered by King Charles I to march his forces to Shrewsbury, so prisoners were exchanged in Manchester and the siege was raised. The Royalists withdrew without compensation, and the Parliamentarians hailed their first victory of the Civil War. Parliament commended Manchester on its achievement, Manchester became the Parliamentarians' main base in Lancashire and ultimately Manchester was allowed one Member of Parliament as a reward for its loyalty to the Commonwealth. Meanwhile, the Royalists may have lost some support in Lancashire as a result of the transfer of Lord Derby and his Lancastrian army to Shrewsbury, since the expectation was that the Lancashire Royalists would defend the King in Lancashire and thereabouts, rather than further afield.

The King's meddling in the allocation and movement of forces was to have a detrimental effect on the campaign. He had already diverted Lord Molyneux to Nottingham, weakening Lord Derby's forces before Manchester. Lord Derby had wanted Charles I to raise his standard at Warrington, with staunch Lancashire Royalists behind him, but Charles chose Nottingham, perhaps an indication of the dislike and distrust of the Stanleys/Derbys felt by the King and his courtiers. It may have been felt that the Stanleys/Derbys had too much power.

The initiative was now with the Parliamentarians. The victorious Manchester garrison destroyed Sir Edward Mosley's Lodge and pacified Bury, where Lord Derby had estates. Royalist Roger Nowell of Read, grandson of Roger Nowell of witch-hunting fame, organized a peace meeting at Blackburn to reconcile the two sides, but neither side would agree to a settlement. The conflict now spread to Blackburn, which was taken by Sir Gilbert Hoghton and his Royalists, who also seized arms at Whalley. The area of East Lancashire incorporating Blackburn, Burnley, Padiham, Colne and Pendle Forest generally sympathized with the Parliamentarian cause. It has been said that the people of the area wanted to feel confident that their crops and livestock would not be pillaged by marauding armies, and a Parliamentarian government was more likely to meet the local population's expectations than a Royalist one – stable government was preferred to cavalier government! Sir Richard Shuttleworth of Gawthorpe Hall was in charge of the Calder Valley Parliamentarians. He met with Charles Towneley of Towneley Hall, Burnley, at Gawthorpe Hall on 17 October 1642, presumably to discuss tactics. Meanwhile, in October 1642, the indecisive Battle of Edgehill was fought, near Banbury in Oxfordshire. Lancastrian Royalists Sir Thomas Tyldesley of Myerscough, Lord Molyneux and Roger Nowell were involved in the conflict.

At the end of 1642, the Royalists controlled, and had garrisons at, Preston, Lancaster, Warrington, Wigan, Brindle and Leigh, but the Parliamentarians were in the ascendancy. In December 1642 Lord Derby was involved in a skirmish at Chowbent, near Leigh, and was forced to retreat. In February 1643, Sir Thomas Fairfax came from Yorkshire to Manchester to initiate a Parliamentarian advance involving Sir John Seaton, Major General of Parliamentarians, Alexander Rigby and Colonel Shuttleworth of Gawthorpe with his East Lancashire detachment, together with the 'Manchester Men', an army raised in Manchester and Bolton. They successfully attacked Bolton, Blackburn and Preston, the last of these being the new Royalist headquarters (their previous headquarters was at Warrington). At Preston, the Parliamentarians forced their way into Church Street and took the town after a fierce two-hour battle, with over 200 Royalists killed. Parliamentarian casualties were only slight. Preston's Mayor Adam Morte and his son were killed but Sir Gilbert Hoghton escaped. Ladies Hoghton and Girlington were apprehended.

Later in February 1643, the Royalists surrendered Hoghton Tower, between Preston and Blackburn. The Hoghton complex comprised hall buildings and a prominent tower which was apparently used to store gunpowder, among other things. The tower blew up, killing Captain Starkey and sixty Parliamentarians, probably as a result of carelessness among the troops, who were still fresh from the soldierly revels following the fall of Preston. Smoking may well have been the cause of the explosion. As is often the case, and despite Parliamentarians tending to lean towards Puritanism, the behaviour of the troops no doubt left something to be desired. The Parliamentarians moved on, taking Lancaster Castle, from which Sir John Girlington escaped.

Lord Derby struck back in the same month, attacking Bolton from Wigan. There was a sharp fight at the Bradshawgate defences and the Royalists burnt a few houses, but Captain Assheton (Sir Ralph Assheton of Middleton), forced them to retreat. Middleton, Oldham, Rochdale and Manchester sent men to support the Bolton Parliamentarians, after Lord Derby had retired to Wigan.

On 4 March 1643, a Spanish galleon with ammunition for the Parliamentarians entered the Wyre Estuary, looking for a place to dock. Lord Derby burnt the galleon, but not completely, and captured a Mr Townson of Lancaster, the Parliamentarian on board. Some of the canon survived the burning, and Colonel George Dodding of Conishead Priory and a detachment of Parliamentarians hurried from Preston to seize the guns, which they shipped up the River Lune to Lancaster Castle. Lord Derby tried but failed to take Lancaster Castle, so the town was pillaged and burned. Sir John Seaton, Colonel Assheton and a Parliamentarian force marched from Preston to relieve Lancaster, but Lord Derby doubled back and took Preston in their absence, after a two-hour skirmish with the depleted garrison at Friargate Bar. Grooms apparently boosted the Royalist cause by locking the Parliamentarians' horses in the stables. On 27 March 1643, Royalists again attacked Bolton and were again repulsed, Bury men coming to the relief of the Bolton Parliamentarians.

Colonel Assheton returned from Lancaster and marched up the Ribble Valley to Whalley, accompanied by Sir Richard Shuttleworth and his contingent. The Parliamentarians were followed by Lord Derby and his Royalists, who camped at Whalley on 19 April 1643. The Royalists had been ordered by Charles I to proceed into Yorkshire, despite being badly needed in Lancashire to defend against further Parliamentarian advances and possibly try to regain lost territory. Charles' grasp of military strategy and tactics once again proved to be limited. Assheton's Parliamentarians paused at the old Read Bridge over Sabden Brook, on the old road from Whalley to Padiham and Burnley. It may be that the Parliamentarians prepared an ambush for the Royalists, or they may have sent a scouting party to seek out the foe, which task they successfully accomplished. It may even have been an accidental musket discharge by a Parliamentarian that surprised the Royalists. Whatever the case, the two sides met and a skirmish ensued. It was a relatively small encounter, but the Royalists were surprised, and, fearing an ambush, they immediately retreated in disarray. The local terrain probably exacerbated the Royalists' problems. The leading troops, turning on a narrow road in a wooded valley, would have caused logistical chaos among the legions behind, who would not have been entirely aware of the nature of the threat. Lord Derby was not a great military tactician and was unable or unwilling to regroup and stem the retreat. Some of his army took shelter in the ruins of Whalley Abbey.

Assheton and Shuttleworth continued to Padiham, but subsequently exploited the Royalists' disarray, killing 300 Royalists and gradually recovering all the lost towns and territory, including Preston and Wigan. Parliamentarian Sir William Brereton and the Manchester Men laid siege to Warrington for three days, and, although he had to withdraw, Colonel Norris of Speke was obliged to surrender the town as his position was untenable. Liverpool was already Parliamentarian, and Lord Derby failed to capture its magazine. In late April, Ralph Assheton relieved Lancaster and had the Spanish guns removed to Manchester.

He took Hornby Castle in the Lune Valley. Also in the Lune Valley, Colonel Alexander Rigby took Thurland Castle from Sir John Girlington with men from Salford and some from Blackburn. They first had to chase off Royalists from Westmorland, Cartmel and Furness. Four hundred prisoners were taken, including Colonel Huddlestone of Millom. Girlington was granted safe passage on surrendering the castle, which was subsequently demolished.

In June 1643, following these setbacks, Charles' wife, Queen Henrietta Maria, ordered Lord Derby to the Isle of Man to guard against rumoured attack from the Scots and to quell local unrest there. It may be that another reason for removing him from the mainland was the previously mentioned distrust and dislike of the Earl among his fellow Royalists, and this was a means of moving him out of the way. Had he been an accomplished general he might have been able to resist his detractors, but he was not, as demonstrated by the recent debacle in the Ribble Valley. The Isle of Man had been a Stanley/Derby domain for a long time and he moved into the family home at Rushen Castle, Castletown, leaving his wife, the Countess, in Lathom.

In the Royalist heartland of Lancashire, only Derby's Lathom House and Greenhalgh Castle, near Garstang, remained in Royalist hands. A degree of anarchy reigned in Lancashire. Wigan was plundered by Colonel Rosworm's Parliamentarians, and Royalist Lord Molyneux and Colonel Thomas Tyldesley in the Fylde plundered Kirkham, Clifton, St Michael's on Wyre and Layton. Royalists raided East Lancashire but were defeated by Sir Richard Shuttleworth's detachment at Colne in July/August 1643. Liverpool lost its Irish trade and Lancashire went hungry, so much so that Parliament offered some financial assistance in September 1644.

Parliamentarian Manchester Men suffered a set-back in Yorkshire in June 1643 but, led by Sir Thomas Fairfax, they survived to defeat an army of Irish Royalists at Nantwich in Cheshire in January 1644. On 24 February 1644, Parliamentarians in Manchester decided to launch an attack on Lathom House, Lord Derby's stronghold. Lathom House was defended by the spirited Lady Derby, who 'held the fort' during her husband's absence in the Isle of Man. The Siege of Lathom is an important event in the history of Lancashire, and is a heroic tale. The Derby family was almost royalty itself in the North, and able to raise and lead a substantial army in the name of King Charles. It was important for the Parliamentarians to suppress the Derby powerhouse at Lathom.

The Earl of Derby's posting to the Isle of Man appears to have been something of a royal tactical blunder, since Lord Derby had a loyal following in Lancashire that would have been more valuable to the hard-pressed King Charles I during the Civil War with Lord Derby at its head than without him. In his absence, his wife was left to defend Lathom House and protect their children. Lady Derby was high-born, of French royal lineage. Her father was the Duke de Tremouille. Her mother was Charlotte Brabantin de Nassau, daughter of Prince William of Orange and Charlotte de Bourbon of the French royal house. Her spirit and strength of character certainly did justice to the family name.

The Parliamentarians were led by Colonel Alexander Rigby of Preston, MP for Wigan, Colonel Ralph Assheton of Middleton, Colonel John Moore of Bankhall, Warrington and Colonel Morgan. They took up their positions on 27 February and a letter from Sir Thomas Fairfax was delivered to the Countess, requiring her submission. She famously refused, and a siege was initiated, the aim being to starve out the defenders. When this failed, they commenced to bombard the house and take it by force. Lathom House was well-provisioned, moated, had walls 6ft thick and had nine towers, housing guns and snipers. In the centre of the complex was the Eagle Tower, the highest of the towers (the eagle features in the Derby crest). High ground to the north, east, south and south-west prevented the besiegers from establishing a battery at a safe distance to bombard the house. The Parliamentarians built a protective trench close to the house, with the assistance of forcibly-recruited local labourers, but the snipers from the towers were a constant irritation. The main Parliamentarian camp was thought to have been located in a wooded dell, subsequently called Cromwell's Trench.

300 defenders faced 2,000 to 3,000 besiegers. Lady Derby was well served by Captains Henry Ogle, Edward Chisnall, Edward Rawsthorne, William Farmer, Mullineux Radcliffe and Richard Fox, and well advised by William Farrington of Werden. On several occasions, the defenders sallied forth from the house to seize arms, much needed provisions and the canon and mortars which presented a serious threat to the fortress.

Several further letters were delivered to the Countess, seeking her submission. She replied to one letter that she 'would rather burn in a fire more merciful than Rigby', and the siege continued. The besiegers continued to try to breach the walls. Their mortars lobbed large stones high into the air, to land within the house walls. There were also grenadoes, hollow iron balls filled with gunpowder, with a burning fuse, which were lobbed into the house, with the object of burning the defenders out. Fire parties in the house defended against the grenadoes, smothering the fires, so that the attackers' ploy did not succeed, and eventually a sally from the house seized the offending mortars. On 5 April Colonels Assheton and Moore resorted to religious tactics, requesting prayers in the churches of Lancashire to enlist the help of God in bringing the siege to a successful conclusion and urging their supporters to cooperate towards that end.

After three months and the loss of 500 besiegers, the Parliamentarians were able to intercept a letter from the Earl of Derby to Lady Derby, advising her that the Royalists, under Prince Rupert (nephew of Charles I, grandson of James I), had defeated the Parliamentarians at Newark and would arrive at Lathom in two days time to relieve the garrison. The consequence was that when, on 27 May, Captains Ogle and Rawsthorne led a sally from Lathom House, they found that their besiegers had departed the previous day. Only six of the Countess's men were lost during the defence of Lathom; 107 cannonballs had been aimed at the house,

32 stones from mortars and just 4 grenadoes. It was a stunning victory for the Royalists, but not one that was to win the Civil Wars. In 1645 the house was again besieged, whilst the Earl and his Lady were in the Isle of Man. The garrison held out for some time, but were eventually starved into submission, the last Royalist stronghold to be suppressed in Lancashire. Following the siege, Cromwell ordered the dismantling of the house and it seems that no authentic drawing of Lathom House has survived.

Lord Derby, having returned from the Isle of Man to Chester in March 1644, had urged Prince Rupert to enter Lancashire and relieve Lathom House. Charles I agreed to allow Prince Rupert to campaign in Lancashire, but it was not until 25 May that Rupert took Stockport and entered the county. He bypassed Manchester, strongly held by Sir John Meldrum, met Lord Derby and Sir Thomas Tyldesley, and proceeded to attack Bolton. The Bolton garrison, together with Colonel Rigby's Parliamentarians who had just withdrawn from the siege of Lathom House, numbered only 2,500 men in total. They resisted the first assault gallantly but could not hold the town. If the defence of Lathom House by the Royalists was one of the brightest features of Lancashire history, the sack of Bolton by the Royalists on 28 May 1644 was one of the darkest, with 1,500 Parliamentarians massacred, including some civilians. Although Lord Derby may have tried to stop civilian deaths, he was blamed for the massacre. Rigby escaped the carnage, but Colonel Shuttleworth's East Lancashire detachment was badly mauled.

Lord Derby and Prince Rupert, grandson of James I, nephew of Charles I, cousin to Charles II and James II, and kinsman to the Countess in their European line, proceeded to Lathom House the same evening, and the scene must have been both jubilant and, for the Derby's, an emotional reunion. Rupert subsequently swept through Lancashire, winning back much territory. He besieged Liverpool for several weeks, but Colonel John Moore and his garrison defended valiantly and were well-stocked. Colonel Clifton had, for instance, taken sheep from Layton Hawes

(Bispham) as provisions for the Parliamentarians. Moore and most of the defenders eventually escaped by sea with their armaments. Some Liverpudlians complained that they had been betrayed by Moore but he said he only withdrew, after a stout defence, when his men refused to fight on. Prince Rupert took Liverpool Castle and the town.

After visiting the Derbys at Lathom, Prince Rupert proceeded via Blackburn, where he defeated Colonel Shutleworth's men in June 1644, and up the Ribble Valley, past Clitheroe and Downham, into Yorkshire. A detachment of his army seized Clitheroe Castle. Some of his army proceeded through the Calder Valley, via Burnley and Colne. There were skirmishes at Haggate, near Burnley, on 24 June, and at Colne, where Colonel Shuttleworth was defeated and wounded. The Royalist armies met up at Skipton and moved on to relieve the Royalists in York. The pivotal battle at Marston Moor, west of York, was fought on 2 July 1644. Prince Rupert and the Royalists, including Lord Derby and his Lancastrian contingent, were defeated by the Parliamentarians, led by General Fairfax and Oliver Cromwell. Prince Rupert retreated into Westmorland and Cumberland. One party of Royalists, led by Sir Marmaduke Langdale, was involved in skirmishes in Craven, as they retreated, and Clitheroe Castle was evacuated by the Royalists after only six weeks.

Lord Derby survived Marston Moor and retreated into south-west Lancashire. He tried to relieve the Royalist garrison under siege at Liverpool, but was badly beaten. Liverpool subsequently surrendered to Sir John Meldrum on 1 November 1644. Lord and Lady Derby fled to the safety of the Isle of Man, where they bided their time in less-violent pursuits, such as horse racing, where a silver cup was competed for, possibly the precursor of the Derby horse race, founded by 12th Earl of Derby in 1780. (It should be noted that the Derby family took its name from the Hundred of West Derby, in south-west Lancashire, and, therefore, that the Derby horse-race is indirectly named after West Derby, and not the city of Derby).

Parliament now dominated Lancashire. Greenhalgh Castle, near Garstang, was taken from the Derbys and destroyed. General Egerton, with 4,000 men, commenced the second siege of Lathom House in July 1645, while Lord and Lady Derby were in Isle of Man. As mentioned, the house was surrendered on 4 December 1645, having run out of supplies, and was dismantled. Cromwell strengthened Parliamentarian forces in Lancashire and there were skirmishes in Ormskirk, Up Holland, Preston and the Wigan area. Elsewhere, Ralph Assheton and Manchester Men fought for Parliament at Naseby, north of Northampton, on 14 June 1645, where Charles I was defeated.

Charles I surrendered in 1646. Sir Thomas Tyldesley of Myerscough surrendered soon after. This was not the end of hostilities, however. The Second Civil War began in 1648 when Charles I promised the Scots that, in return for their support, Presbyterianism would be declared the main religion in England. A Scots army numbering 20,000 invaded England, led by the Duke of Hamilton, and 4,000 English soldiers from north Lancashire and Westmorland joined them, under the command of Sir Marmaduke Langdale. Sir Thomas Tyldesley also joined their ranks.

As the Royalists reached Preston, Oliver Cromwell came in pursuit, entering Lancashire from Yorkshire via Gisburn, where he and his army camped and were joined by Colonel Shuttleworth's Calder Valley contingent. The Parliamentarian army was at Clitheroe on 16 August 1648 and crossed 'Cromwell's Bridge' over the River Hodder, moving on towards Preston via Stoneyhurst. The Parliamentarians intercepted the invaders at Ribbleton Moor, where the four-hour Battle of Preston was fought on 17 August 1648. The Scots army was stretched out, north to south, and Cromwell split them in two, entering Preston. Cromwell, Fairfax and Ralph Assheton pursued the Duke of Hamilton and the Royalist army across Walton Bridge over the Ribble; 1,000 Royalists were killed and 4,000 captured. Hamilton and the southern part of his Scots army continued to escape southwards, plundering Wigan and clashing again with Cromwell at Winwick Green, where they lost another 1,000 men. At Warrington Bridge they made a last stand and were finally vanquished. Hamilton surrendered on terms and proceeded into Cheshire. Meanwhile, the remainder of his army north of Preston had been chased further north for 10 miles and either killed, captured or dispersed.

Charles I surrendered yet again. He was executed on 30 January 1649. Cromwell demanded that Lord Derby surrender the Isle of Man, which was the only part of England, Ireland and Wales still not controlled by Parliament. Lord Derby refused, despite being offered half his estates back if he complied with the demand.

During 1649, Colonel Shuttleworth's men became disgruntled at receiving no pay, and occupied Clitheroe Castle in protest. Their demands were met. Subsequently, Parliament sent Major General Sir John Lambert into Lancashire to disband the forces there, and one of his actions was to dismantle Clitheroe Castle. Cromwell tended to pay soldiers from the sale of lands confiscated from Royalist sympathizers. Many landowners lost part of their lands, as did Edmund Robinson of Hawks House, Reedley, near Burnley, where some of my own relatives lived in the twentieth century.

The execution of Charles I did not mark the end of the Civil Wars. In 1651, Charles II claimed the throne and invaded with a Scottish army through Lancaster, Preston, Chorley and Warrington, pressing on to Worcester. Charles was declared King in Lancaster, but Lancashire Presbyterians did not rush to join him, as he had hoped, and most of Lancashire ignored the army passing through its midst. However, some Royalists did rise to the cause, and Lord Derby returned from the Isle of Man with Manx troops, landing at Rossall Point on the River Wyre estuary on 15 August 1651. Lord Derby proceeded to Lathom, meeting Charles II at Chester. Charles II ordered him to attack the Parliamentarians at Wigan Lane, near Standish, north of Wigan. The Royalists fought well, but were overwhelmed by the Parliamentarians under Colonel Robert Lilburne and Sir John Lambert. Sir Thomas Tyldesley of Myerscough was killed in the fray. Lord Derby lost two horses and was hit by six musket balls, but, though wounded, his armour saved him from more serious injury. He was sheltered by a woman at the Old Dog Inn and was able to join Charles II at Worcester.

The Royalist army was defeated at the Battle of Worcester on 2 December 1651, the last major engagement of the Civil Wars in England. Lord Derby, still handicapped by his wounds, helped Charles II to escape (ultimately to France), but surrendered to Captain Oliver Edge in Nantwich, *en route* to Knowsley, and was imprisoned at Chester. Despite believing that Captain Edge had given him 'quarter for life', which would ensure that he was treated as a prisoner of war, not subject to execution as punishment for his military activities, Lord Derby was court-martialled for treason, found guilty and sentenced to be beheaded at Bolton. The choice of Bolton was significant, this being the place where Lord Derby was deemed to have allowed the massacre to take place following the Battle of Bolton in May 1644. He managed to escape from the confines of Chester Castle by persuading his guards to allow him access to the roof and then descending the wall using a rope supplied by his friends, but he was recaptured in the area of the modern race-course when he apparently mistook enemies for supporters and approached them. Thomas Stanley, 7th Earl of Derby, was beheaded at Bolton on 15 October 1651, having been held at the Man and Scythe Inn in the town. Following his death the distraught Lady Derby surrendered the Isle of Man to Parliament and was made a prisoner there.

The Stanleys/Derbys lost as much from Civil War as any family in England. By supporting the losing side for, perhaps, too long. Thomas, the 7th Earl, lost most of the estates and wealth gained by the astute 1st Earl of Derby, of Bosworth Field fame. The Derby estates were sequestered under the Commonwealth, except for Lathom, Knowsley and a few others belonging to Lady Derby. She was hard up after 7th Earl's death, Parliament refusing to restore her estates, and received little assistance from her son, Charles, the 8th Earl. Another Lancastrian who rose to prominence during the

Commonwealth era was Colonel Worsley of Manchester, the son of a cloth merchant, who helped Cromwell to turn out the Rump Parliament in 1653. Worsley became Major General of the Lancashire District, one of the ten districts into which England was divided under Cromwell's Commonwealth. He was a strict Puritan, closing 200 inns in Blackburn and banning horse-racing. He was rewarded for his loyalty by burial in Westminster Abbey.

Following the execution of the 7th Earl, his son, Charles Stanley, became 8th Earl of Derby. He had married against his parents' wishes and as a result was estranged from them. He became reconciled with his father during the latter's trial and tried gallantly to have his father's death sentence overturned, but was never reconciled with the Countess of Derby, who always disliked his wife. The 8th Earl participated in Sir George Booth's 1658 rising at Warrington, the aim of which was to put Charles II on the throne, but the rising failed after a short, unsuccessful engagement at Nantwich, following which Lord Derby was jailed.

Cromwell's Commonwealth and Protectorate became increasingly unpopular, especially after his death in 1648, when his son, Richard, succeeded him but lacked his personality and military background. In 1660, General Monk and the army restored the Stuarts to the throne in the person of King Charles II (1660-1685). As a measure of how times had changed, Manchester, once the heartland of the Parliamentarians, was jubilant at the Restoration, and there was a festive spirit in the town when Charles II visited Manchester on 22 April 1661. Charles appointed General Monk Duke of Albemarle and awarded him the Honour of Clitheroe, part of the Duchy of Lancaster, which was later inherited by the Dukes of Buccleuch.

If Lancashire Royalists expected Charles to restore their lost estates, they were to be sadly disappointed. The fate of the Derbys exemplifies this. Charles restored the 8th Earl's titles, but not his estates in Lancashire, Cheshire, Yorkshire and elsewhere, despite both Houses of Parliament voting for their restoration. However, the Isle of Man was restored to the Derbys, and the 8th Earl immediately annoyed Charles II by having an islander named William Christian tried, sentenced and shot for collaborating with the Parliamentarians in the handing over of Rushen Castle and the island to the Parliamentarians during the last days of his mother's rule there in 1651. Not only did Charles II feel that the action was extreme, but considered that the monarch's right to review such sentences, before they were carried out, had been breached. However, the 8th Earl was appointed Lord Lieutenant of Lancashire. He was anti-Papist, anti-Puritan and pro-Nonconformist, and was lenient in the application of Charles' laws against Nonconformists in Lancashire. Ironically, Presbyterians were in favour of the Restoration, but soon suffered discrimination, their ministers being ejected from sixty-seven parish churches in Lancashire as they refused to conform to the procedures of the English Church. However, Charles II did allow worship in Nonconformist chapels towards the close of his reign.

Charles II was succeeded by his brother, James II (1685-1688). During James' reign there was general disquiet in the country. James had Catholic leanings. As an example, he deprived the 9th Lord Derby of the Lord Lieutenancy of Lancashire and Cheshire in favour of a Catholic Molyneux. James had a son, James Edward, by his Catholic second wife, Mary of Modena, and there was fear of a Catholic succession in England. The 9th Lord Derby, who was brother to Charles, the 8th Earl, succeeding him in 1672, not surprisingly welcomed the Glorious Revolution of 1688, when James II was ousted and replaced on the throne by William of Orange (King William III, 1688-1702) and Queen Mary, daughter of James II. James was exiled to France, but, with French assistance, he landed in Ireland and was well-received there. William of Orange and his army proceeded to Ireland through Lancashire and defeated James at the Battle of the Boyne in 1691, in reality ending James' hopes of a restoration of the throne.

CAPTAIN MYLES STANDISH AND THE
MAYFLOWER

The Standish family was one of Lancashire's leading families. They marched into battle at Bosworth Field in 1485 under the Stanley banner, but the most famous son of the Standish family, especially in the USA, was Myles Standish, who was born around 1587 in West Lancashire. Incidentally, Myles Standish may well have been christened by William Leigh, a puritanical local preacher who played a judicial role in the trials of the Pendle and Samlesbury Witches at Lancaster. The Standishes of Duxbury had abandoned the Old Faith and seemed to be leaning towards Puritanism. This was certainly the case with Myles Standish.

The Standish family probably had a military background. When Myles Standish was perhaps only fourteen years old he was a drummer boy in the English contingent of the Anglo-Dutch armies fighting Spain in the Low Countries. The Netherlands at that time belonged to Spain, and was striving for independence. Queen Elizabeth sent an English army over to assist England's Protestant ally in its struggle, and there was a significant Lancastrian presence in that army. Standish visited Leyden in the Netherlands and met members of a puritanical separatist movement who had fled England and taken refuge in the more-liberal Netherlands so that they could pursue their lives and religious beliefs without persecution.

Myles Standish became familiar with this separatist sect, who we can now call the Pilgrims, and was invited by them to accompany them to the New World as their military leader. So, as Captain Myles Standish, he and his wife, Rose, sailed with the Pilgrims from Delftshaven in the Netherlands on 21 July 1620 in the *Speedwell*, en route to Southampton, where they met up with the *Mayflower*, which had sailed from London with a further group of Pilgrims. The two ships sailed from Southampton on 5 August 1820, but the *Speedwell* started to leak and both ships had to put into Dartmouth on 12 August for repairs to be made to the *Speedwell*.

It was 23rd August before they recommenced their voyage. Once beyond Lands End the *Speedwell* started to leak dangerously again so the ships turned back and took refuge in Plymouth Harbour, where the decision was taken that the *Speedwell* was unfit for an Atlantic crossing and had to be left behind. Some of the *Speedwell* Pilgrims returned to London, others crowded onto the *Mayflower* and on 6 September 1620 they set sail for the New World once again. The *Mayflower* arrived at Cape Cod on 10 November 1620. They had originally intended to settle in Virginia, but circumstances conspired to push them further north, so they changed their plans.

There is a common misconception that Captain Myles Standish was the captain of the *Mayflower*. He was not. He was a military captain, not a naval one. Captain Christopher Jones was master of the *Mayflower*. On arrival in the new World, she rested at anchor in Cape Cod harbour and the Pilgrims lived on board for some time until a location for their settlement was chosen across the bay, in an area already known as Plymouth. Unfortunately, the wife of Myles Standish, Rose, died on board the *Mayflower* on 29 January 1621. The Pilgrims suffered great hardship and loss of life, but pressed on and built the Plymouth settlement, while Standish organised their defence and made forays into Indian territory. Standish was known as 'Captain Shrimpe' because of his red hair. He was never a Pilgrim, but was sympathetic towards their Puritan beliefs. Ten years after the founding of the Plymouth settlement a second settlement was founded a few miles north and was named Duxbury, after Duxbury Hall in Lancashire, home of one branch of the Standish family, in honour of Myles Standish, who was a leading light in the settlement and returned once to England in 1626 on settlement business.

Some time after Rose Standish died Standish married a second wife, Barbara, who arrived, quite appropriately, on the *Rose* in 1623. Little is known about the two wives of Myles Standish, not even their maiden names, but it is possible that they were related to each other. However, before the arrival of Barbara, tradition has it that Myles set his eye upon Priscilla Mullins, whose parents had recently died. This tradition was recorded for posterity by Henry Wadsworth Longfellow in 1858 in his epic poem *The Courtship of Miles Standish*, and thus the place of Myles Standish in American history was assured. I myself have explored the town of Duxbury in Massachusetts, and paddled on Duxbury Beach, and climbed the Standish Monument on Captain's Hill, Duxbury. Longfellow's poem says of Myles Standish that:

> He was a gentleman born, could trace his pedigree plainly
> Back to Hugh Standish of Duxbury Hall, in Lancashire, England,
> Who was the son of Ralph, and the grandson of Thurston de Standish;
> Heir unto vast estates, of which he was basely defrauded.

No doubt with much poetic licence, Longfellow relates how Standish asked his friend John Alden to approach Priscilla Mullins and advise her of Myles' interest in her as a future wife. John Alden faithfully did as he was asked, but Priscilla's answer was in the negative, so John Alden did some courting on his own behalf and ended up marrying Priscilla Mullins himself. So much for friendship! These scenes are sometimes portrayed in plays by young American schoolchildren at Thanksgiving. Whatever the truth of the courtship story, Myles Standish and John Alden remained good friends. Myles and his second wife, Barbara, brought up a family. Myles Standish died in 1656. His successors, much later, tried to reclaim the estates of which Longfellow says he was defrauded, but with no success.

CHAPTER FIVE

WILLIAM AND MARY, THE HANOVERIANS AND THE '15 AND '45 REBELLIONS, 1688-1745

THE LANCASHIRE PLOT, 1694

There was some opposition in England, not least in Lancashire, to the Glorious Revolution of 1688, which removed King James II from the English throne and sent him into exile. William of Orange was disliked as a foreigner, and Queen Mary as a usurper of her father's throne. Additionally, there was still some sympathy among the Royalists of Lancashire towards the Stuarts, despite a feeling that the Stuarts had not exactly shown gratitude to their Lancastrian supporters, for instance in terms of restoring lands confiscated by the Parliamentarians.

In this scenario, it was not surprising, perhaps, that villains should try to exploit the situation. So it was that the trial began on 20 October 1694 of certain members of the Lancashire gentry accused of plotting the overthrow of William and Mary and the reinstatement of James II, the so-called Lancashire Plot. It was also not surprising that the people of Manchester, where the trial was held, largely sympathised with the plight of the 'plotters', given the lack of popularity of the monarchs and the suspicions of the townsfolk that the accusers of the 'plotters' were corrupt.

Already, in 1693, a commission had sat in Warrington to consider accusations against certain Catholic Lancastrians

(Caryll, 3rd Lord Molyneux, William Standish, Thomas Eccleston, William Dicconson, Sir Nicholas Sherburne, Sir William Gerrard and Thomas Gerrard) that they had illegally allocated lands and/or income for the benefit of the Catholic faith, but the evidence had been seen to be untrustworthy and the accused acquitted. Had they been convicted, their estates would have been confiscated and one-third of them awarded to the accusers – an incentive, indeed, for the lodging of unjust accusations.

In the 1694 trial, Sir Roland Stanley, Sir Thomas Clifton, William Dicconson, Philip Langton and William Blundell were accused of the more serious crime of plotting to murder William of Orange and to reinstate James II. Lord Molyneux, Sir William Gerrard and Bartholomew Walmsley were accused separately. Conviction could lead to execution. The chief witness was John Lunt, who alleged that he and others were tasked to elicit commissions from James II to be distributed among the Lancashire Jacobites, including the accused, preparatory to an uprising, and that he was also to ferment dissatisfaction in the North in favour of James II. Various other revelations emerged, including a claim that

James II was have to re-entered England through Lancashire to reclaim the throne in 1692 but was delayed by the defeat of the French fleet by the English at The Hague. The defence witnesses had their say, trashing the character of John Lunt and characterising him as a scoundrel, a bigamist and a highwayman. Witnesses testified that Lunt had offered payments to them in return for helping to denounce the gentry and that Lunt had been involved in another case in Kent, similar to the Lancashire one, where Lunt had failed to provide evidence against his intended victims.

The judge, in his summing up, said that the matter deserved grave consideration, but the jury merely consulted each other and found the defendants not guilty without leaving the court. In dismissing the defendants, the judge again showed his bias by telling them that the Government was a merciful and easy one, and that they should avoid plots and conspiracies! 'Not guilty, but don't do it again,' he seemed to be saying. In dismissing the case against Lord Molyneux, Sir William Gerrard and Bartholomew Walmsley, where no evidence was presented, the judge told them to 'go and sin no more!' As a result of the false accusations against him, Lord Molyneux lost his position as Constable of Liverpool Castle, a title his family had held since the fifteenth century.

The people of Manchester were delighted, and drummed Lunt and his henchmen out of town. Fishwick claims that the acquitted gentlemen accused Lunt and two others of perjury and they were found guilty at Lancaster Assizes, although Axon notes that the perjurers were never convicted, but were at least prevented from repeating their accusations against others across the country, which they would have done had they succeeded in Manchester. Strangely, a resolution of the House of Commons, some time later, declared that there had been a dangerous plot and that the prosecution had been justified, but this may have been a purely political statement.

THE HOUSE OF HANOVER AND THE 1715 JACOBITE REBELLION

When King James II died in exile in France in 1701, his son, James Edward Stuart, the Old Pretender, was recognised as King James III of England by Louis XIV of France, much to the chagrin of King William (William III) and his Government. The Old Pretender and his Jacobite followers had not given up hope of replacing William on the English throne (Jacobite being derived from 'Jacobus', the Latin name for James). There was strong support in Lancashire for a Jacobite restoration, since Catholics and High Church members tended to believe that the monarch ruled by Divine Right, and that the removal of the Stuarts in 1688 was unlawful. Catholics had generally been loyal to the Stuarts throughout the Civil Wars. They remembered the long period of persecution under the Protestant Tudors and disliked William of Orange's Protestantism and the favouritism he displayed towards Nonconformists. Low Church members and Dissenters were more likely to be loyal to William of Orange and the Whig Government, especially so given that William's Toleration Act of 1689 was aimed at Dissenters.

William of Orange died in 1702, leaving no heirs. His wife, Queen Mary, predeceased him, in 1694. Mary's sister, Anne, another daughter of James II, succeeded to the throne as Queen Anne (1702-1714), but she also left no heirs, and so it was that George, of the House of Hanover, son of Sophia (granddaughter of James I) and Ernest Augustus (Elector of Hanover) became King George I (1714-1727). When Queen Anne died in 1714 the Jacobites saw an opportunity for a Stuart restoration. They were greatly disappointed when George I became King. He was one-quarter Stuart, being the great-grandson of James I, nephew of Prince Rupert of Civil War fame, but that was not sufficient for the Jacobites. Further, George did not speak English, was not immediately popular among his new subjects and continued to implement the Toleration Act. On the Old Pretender's birthday, Friday, 10 June 1715, a Manchester mob drank the health of King James and, led by a blacksmith called Thomas Sydall, ravaged Manchester for several days, wrecking the Dissenters' chapel in Acresfield, later known as Cross Street Unitarian Chapel, and meeting houses in Monton, Blackley, and elsewhere. The mob had the tacit encouragement of some magistrates with Jacobite sympathies. There was mob violence elsewhere in the country, too.

In Manchester, the Earl of Stair quelled the mob with the military, and the situation returned to normal. Sydall and his colonel were tried at Lancaster, put in the stocks, although the public were forbidden from throwing things at them, and sent back to prison. The rioters were more likely to be High Churchmen, Catholics and troublemakers. Many High Church members were more inclined to posture than to rebel, but, together with the Catholics, they offered the hope of 20,000 Lancastrians rising in support of a Jacobite rebellion, should there be one. Jacobite clubs had sprung up in Lancashire, meeting seemingly innocuously in inns, and the mock 'town corporation' of Walton-le-Dale, meeting in the Unicorn Inn and shadowing the legitimate town ruling body, may have been a cover for pro-Jacobite activities.

The Scots Jacobites were more intent on fighting for Scotland's independence, and would have been better advised to restrict their campaign to Scotland. Some Highlanders deserted, rather than roaming south of the border, but the rebel army moved through Cumberland and Westmorland into Lancashire. They were joined by the Earl of Derwentwater, who had raised an army in the north, and, incidentally, was a member of the mock 'town corporation' of Walton-le-Dale. Edward Tyldesley of Myerscough, John Dalton of Thurnham Hall, near Lancaster, Albert Hodgson and Richard Butler of Rawcliffe Hall also joined the rising, but the level of support in Lancashire was low and the populace tended to distance themselves from the invaders, despite earlier indications of the popularity of the Jacobite cause.

The rebels were incompetently led. Their most-experienced leader, Brigadier Mackintosh, knew that their mission was hopeless from the start. But they had been expected to take the East Coast route to Newcastle, where the main English force was moving to check them, so they were unopposed in North Lancashire. Sir Henry Hoghton, of Hoghton Tower was charged with the defence of North Lancashire, but he and his loyal troops were outnumbered and withdrew to Preston.

Colonel Charteris of Hornby Castle, a sharpster, was also charged with the defence of North Lancashire, but was somewhat incompetent, commencing to destroy the bridge over the Lune at Lancaster, but then realising that the river was fordable at low tide! Charteris was a merchant, responsible for the development of the port at Sunderland Point. He tried to buy six guns from Robert Lawson, a Quaker, but Lawson feared that the rebels would damage his ship if they discovered that he had sold guns to the Government forces, so he requested a £10,000 bond as insurance against this eventuality. Charteris would not agree to the bond and ordered Lawson offshore, to keep the guns out of the rebels' hands. Lawson disobeyed the order, and the rebels subsequently seized the guns.

The rebels reached Kirkby Lonsdale on 6 November 1715 and entered Lancaster on 7 November. They released prisoners from Lancaster Castle, including Thomas Sydall, the Manchester riot leader, who joined their cause. James III was declared King at the market cross in Lancaster, in his absence (he was still in France). After dallying and socialising for two nights in Lancaster, where the atmosphere was somewhat festive and where each night was graced with a ball, the rebels moved south on 9 November, taking the brandy from the customs house with them and consuming it before they reached Garstang! Some of the foot-soldiers stayed overnight in Garstang, while the mounted troops moved on. The rebels occupied Preston, Hoghton's small army having vacated the town, awaiting the arrival of General Carpenter and the main force from Newcastle. The Pretender was proclaimed King once again, at Preston Cross, and the rebels dallied and socialised for three days. As with Lancaster, the ladies of Preston seem to have been impressed by their

gay visitors. It has been said that: 'The ladies of this town,
Preston, are so very beautiful and so richly attired, that the
gentlemen-soldiers from Wednesday to Saturday minded
nothing but courting and feasting'.

Only a couple of townsfolk joined the rebels in Lancaster
and not many more joined in Preston. No High Church
members joined, but several members of the Catholic gentry
were recruited in Preston, including Richard Towneley, Sir
Francis Anderton of Lostock, Richard Chorley of Chorley,
Ralph Standish of Standish, John Leybourn of Nateby, near
Garstang, and Gabriel Hesketh of Whitehill, Goosnargh.

General Wills approached with Government forces via
Manchester, where he left 1,000 men to control the disaf-
fected population, some High Churchmen fleeing, some
being arrested there and others keeping their heads down.
Wills took charge of the Government forces approaching
Preston, while the rebels, led by General Forster and numbering only 4,000, dallied, lacking strategy and objectives.
It was at this point that the brave Church of England curate,
Samuel Peploe, later to become Bishop of Chester, said the
normal prayers for King George and his family during a
service in the parish church, despite the attendance of some
rebel cavaliers. The rebels threatened to do him harm unless
he prayed for 'King James', at which Peploe is said to have
replied, 'Soldiers, I am doing my duty; do you do yours',
and continued with the service, unmolested. Peploe gained
praise from George I himself, who, hearing that his name
was 'Peep-low', commented that 'he shall peep high; I will
make him a bishop'. Other sturdy Lancastrians rallied to the
loyal cause. Wills had invited Sir Henry Hoghton to raise a
detachment of troops. Hoghton wrote to Revd James Woods
of Chowbent and Revd Woods (later nicknamed 'General'
Woods), John Walton of Horwich, John Turner of Preston
and other local clergymen sought local volunteers and took
them and their improvised weapons to fight the invaders.

On Saturday, 12 November, General Wills and Sir Henry
Hoghton reached Walton-le-Dale and the River Ribble. They
surprised the rebels, attacking from the south. Brigadier

Mackintosh advised that the rebels should abandon Walton Bridge and build barricades in Preston, at Church Street, Lancaster Road, Friargate and Fishergate, to aid the defence of the town. This was done. General Wills attacked the barricades the same day, first at Church Street then at Fishergate, and there was some initial heavy fighting: Wills' attacking force sustained heavy losses and were repulsed. However, the next day, Sunday, General Carpenter's army arrived from the North-east, via the Ribble Valley, and the rebels found themselves surrounded. General Forster sued for terms, but Wills demanded unconditional surrender, declaring, 'I will not treat with rebels', while the Highlanders were disinclined to surrender and were involved in further skirmishes. Many rebels escaped northwards, through the Government cordon, but the surrender came on 13 November 1715. The rebels' swords were deposited at the churchyard and the Mitre Inn and 1,569 prisoners taken, 1,000 of them Scots. The rebels lost fewer than 200 dead in the fighting. Preston suffered damage and looting at the hands of the victorious Government forces, following the collapse, despite most of its population being loyal to George I.

Following the surrender in Preston market place, many of the rebel prisoners were corralled in the parish church, but rebel officers and gentlemen were detained at the Mitre, White Bull and Windmill Inns; 400 prisoners were taken to Lancaster Castle, and on this occasion they were ignored by the ladies of the town! 200 men remained imprisoned there for a year, of whom fifty died and the rest were transported to the West Indies; 100 prisoners were sent to Liverpool, for trial. A total of forty rebels were executed, including twenty-four Lancastrians. The executions were spread around the county, for maximum effect, with five in Manchester, four in Liverpool, seven in Wigan, twelve in Preston, four in Garstang and four in Lancaster. Thomas Sydall was one of the five hanged, drawn and quartered at Knott Mill, Manchester, on 11 February 1716 for his part in the mob violence of 1714. The leaders of the rebellion were sent to London for trial. The Earl of Derwentwater was beheaded.

John Dalton of Thurnham, Ralph Standish of Standish and Albert Hodgson of Leighton Hall were imprisoned, but were released on payment of heavy fines. Apparently, the ruined John Dalton walked back to Thurnham Hall, to find his wife collecting sticks and his house in a dilapidated state. Richard Towneley and Sir Francis Anderton were acquitted of the charges against them. Nicholas Blundell of Little Crosby, a Catholic and an enlightened gentleman farmer, was suspected of involvement in the rebellion, probably because anti-Catholic feeling was running high. After the surrender, he left Crosby for a two-year sojourn in London, Douai and Rome.

The Old Pretender landed at Perth in January 1716, too late to salvage anything from the rebellion.

PRINCE CHARLES EDWARD STUART'S SUPPOSED VISIT TO MANCHESTER, 1744

To put this story in context, it will be remembered that the last of our Stuart kings, James II, ruled from 1685 to 1688, when he was deposed in the 'Glorious Revolution', sent into exile and replaced on the throne by William of Orange and Mary (daughter to James II). James died in exile in 1701, but his son, James Edward Stuart, sometimes called James III but usually known as the Old Pretender, continued to aspire to the English throne from foreign lands. The 1715 incursion from Scotland was quelled and was followed in 1720 by the birth of James Edward's son, Charles Edward Stuart, the Young Pretender, Bonnie Prince Charlie.

The next milestone in the struggle to reinstate the Stuarts was the 1745 rebellion, but, preparatory to that event, Bonnie Prince Charlie visited Manchester in disguise to investigate the support that he might expect from the residents when the invasion came, or so the tradition has it. The visit was recorded in a rhyme in Aston's *Metrical Records of Manchester*, which indicates that promises come easy, commitments do not:

No doubt he was promised an army! a host!
Tho' he found, to his cost, it was a vain boast:
For when he returned, in the year forty-five,
For the crown of his Fathers, in person to strive...
The hope he had cherished from promises made
Remain to this day as a debt that's unpaid.

The Young Pretender supposedly stayed at Ancoats Hall, home of Sir Oswald Mosley, for several weeks. There is no formal record in the Mosley archives about the visit, but Sir Oswald, in his *Family Memoirs* of 1849, recounts a tale told to a Mr Aston and later related to him by Aston. An old lady who died in Manchester in 1815, aged eighty-four, had told Aston many times that when she was thirteen, in 1744, and living with her father, named Bradbury, at Manchester's chief inn in Market Street, a handsome man came every post-day for several weeks to read the newspapers. There were three post-days a week, and on those days newspapers were delivered to the inn from London, the inn being the chief receiving point for newspapers. The stranger read the papers and talked to no one, but on his last visit asked for a bowl of water and a towel, which she delivered and received half-a-crown for her pains.

The next year, as she watched Bonnie Prince Charlie march into town at the head of his army, she recognised him as the handsome gentleman of 1744, and told her father, who took her indoors and threatened her, telling her never to repeat what she had said. He repeated his threats often after the retreat of the Scots. Her father later confirmed that it had indeed been the Prince who had visited the inn to read the papers.

Axon is dismissive of these claims. Apart from the fact that the visit would have been dangerous and of little political value, the alleged visit in 1744 was not recorded by any of the main Jacobite sympathisers in the town, John Byrom, the Claytons or the Deacons, and there is no other firm evidence to back the claim. Axon's conclusion is that the visit never happened.

THE HOUSE OF HANOVER AND THE
1745 JACOBITE REBELLION

King George II (1727-1760), like his father, George I, had to contend with a Jacobite rebellion, the '45. The Scots were encouraged by the French to harry the English and to try to install Bonnie Prince Charlie on the throne. The Prince landed in the western Highlands of Scotland in June 1745, crossed Scotland and marched into Edinburgh, defeating a Government army at Prestonpans, just east of Edinburgh in September. The Duke of Cumberland, son of George II, was sent to the Midlands to command the defences there and General Wade was despatched to Northumberland, where the invading army was expected to enter England. However, Bonnie Prince Charlie and the rebels invaded in the west. The people of Lancaster and elsewhere in Lancashire generally ignored or avoided him and his army.

As in 1715, the rebels proceeded to Preston, but on this occasion there was no languishing. Bonnie Prince Charlie slept at the house of Nicholas Starkie, in Market Street, and promptly continued his march south. He gained little support in Preston. Warrington Bridge had been demolished, so the rebels marched to Manchester, instead of Wigan. Many of the residents of Manchester evacuated the town, with their belongings.

200 or 300 volunteers joined the rebels in Manchester, this detachment being termed the 'Manchester Regiment', led by Colonel Francis Towneley. They forded the river at Stockport and continued south. As in 1715, Henry Hoghton raised a militia in Lancashire in support of the Government, but his force was not involved in any conflict.

John Byrom, the Lancashire poet, met Bonnie Prince Charlie in Manchester under sufferance, given that he did not want to be associated with the rebellion. Byrom wrote the following ditty, reflecting the thoughts of those who were suffering from confused loyalties:

God bless the King, of Church and State defender;
God bless (no harm in blessing) the Pretender;
But who Pretender is and who the King,
God bless us all! That's quite another thing.

Bonnie Prince Charlie and his force of 10,000 penetrated as far south as Swarkestone Bridge over the River Trent, just to the south of Derby. Against his better judgement, he was persuaded by his commanders to retreat northwards, as the two Government armies were converging on him, General Wade from the north and the Duke of Cumberland from the southwest. The trap was closing rapidly. By 7 December 1745, the Prince and the rebels were back in Manchester. They reached Preston on 12 December and left Lancaster on 15 December, having plundered the town, chased by General Oglethorpe. In Liverpool, a Protestant mob showed their contempt for the rebels by destroying a Catholic chapel.

Colonel Francis Towneley of Towneley, Burnley, and the Manchester Regiment defended Carlisle in a rearguard action, but their defence was in vain and by 30 December all the rebels in the town were either dead or had surrendered. Towneley was executed. Thomas Coppock from Manchester, chaplain to Bonnie Prince Charlie, who had been appointed Bishop of Carlisle by the Prince, was hanged drawn and quartered, as were Thomas Deacon of Manchester and Thomas Sydall, son of Thomas Sydall of Manchester who had been executed after the 1715 uprising. It is somewhat surprising that such barbaric punishments were meted out as late as 1745.

The rebellion ended with the massacre at Culloden, north of Inverness, on 16 April 1746. After a six-month sojourn in the Western Isles, Bonnie Prince Charlie escaped to France, accompanied by Sir John Towneley, brother to Colonel Francis.

THE LATER HANOVERIANS

King George II died in 1760. His eldest son, Frederick, Prince of Wales, pre-deceased him, so Frederick's son became King George III (1760-1820). It was in the reign of George III that Lancastrians were able to get a better view of their county, if only representationally. In 1786, William Yates, of Liverpool, a mapper working in the Custom House, issued his county map of Lancashire. His map was produced by a team of surveyors who used innovative procedures during his survey, the main one being triangulation, which, although not new, had reached new levels of accuracy. Yates established two sea-beach base lines of 10 and 6 miles length, which he was able to measure with great accuracy. These base lines were probably from Formby to North Meols and from Formby to Bootle. The Formby-North Meols line was the base line of the initial triangle. Yates' survey teams then spread out over the whole of Lancashire, establishing three trigonometrical principal stations, Warton Crag, Pendle and Billinge Beacon, followed by twenty-eight other stations, from which the whole of Lancashire was triangulated. Local detail was added from various sources, including local topographical surveys and contemporary local maps. Yates' legacy to Lancashire was the creation of one of the best county maps of the eighteenth century, as befits the county leading Britain through the Industrial Revolution.

Another feature of the reigns of George II and George III was the development of the Shaker movement in Manchester. The Shakers were so named because of the trembling fits of religious ecstasy that they experienced during devotions. They believed in a second coming, as reflected in their formal name, the United Society of Believers in Christ's Second Appearing, William E.A. Axon tells the story of Ann Lee, the Manchester Prophetess and leader of the Shakers. Mother Ann, as she was known, was born in Toad Lane, Manchester, in 1736, the daughter of a blacksmith. The movement attained a strength of around thirty adherents, but decided to emigrate to the USA and embarked for New York on

19 May 1774. They settled in communes near to Albany, in Upper New York State. Ann Lee died in 1784, aged forty-eight, and James Whittaker, a native of Oldham, took over as leader of the Shakers. The movement reached a peak of 6,000 adherents in twenty-four communities, but barely survives to the present day, having ceased to accept any new converts in 1965. Its communities in New York State, New England and elsewhere were, over the years, a source of Shaker-style furniture, crafts and farm implements. Today, these communities survive as tourist attractions.

George III was succeeded by his son, George IV (1820-1830), who left no surviving heirs. His brother, William, succeeded to the throne as King William IV (1830-1837), but he, too, left no heirs. William's next-oldest brother, Edward, Duke of Kent, had died in 1820, but Edward left an heir, a daughter. Thus it was that Victoria, daughter of Edward, granddaughter of George III and niece to George IV and William IV, came to the throne as Queen Victoria (1837-1901).

These were times of accelerating change in Lancashire, as the modern world emerged. Developments in politics, in industry, especially cotton textiles and coal-mining, in transportation systems, especially canals and railways, and in the population of the county were truly staggering. The following chapters address various aspects of these astonishing times.

CHAPTER SIX

THE REFORM ACT, THE REPEAL OF THE CORN LAWS, LITERARY LANCASHIRE AND THE NINETEENTH CENTURY

LANCASHIRE'S NINETEENTH-CENTURY POLITICIANS

Lancashire's growing economic importance in the nineteenth century was reflected in its growing political importance, with the emergence of individuals who shaped British politics at the highest level. In particular, Sir Robert Peel, John Bright, Richard Cross, Lord Derby and William Gladstone were prominent Lancastrians on the stage of British, and even world, politics.

Sir Robert Peel (1788-1850) was born in Bury. His father, the first Sir Robert Peel, was a successful calico printer with a large factory in Ramsbottom. The elder Sir Robert had already dabbled in politics, sponsoring the 1819 Factory Act which, among other things, forbade children under nine years old from being employed in the mills. The younger Peel entered politics as Member of Parliament for Cashel, my own ancestral town in Tipperary, and became Irish Secretary, then Home Secretary, under the Duke of Wellington, in which posts he founded the Royal Irish constabulary and, in 1829, the London police force, (hence the nicknames bobbies and peelers given to police officers). As Home Secretary, Sir Robert carried out criminal reforms and reforms of the legal and prison systems, among other measures reducing the hideous number of petty crimes for which execution was

Rochdale's John Bright (left), the founder of the Anti-Corn Law League, and his friend, Richard Cobden (right).

the penalty and overhauling the system governing the transportation of criminals. He was leader of the Conservative Party, which he successfully reformed. Queen Victoria considered asking him to form a government in 1839, but, in the so-called Bedchamber crisis, Peel sought a reduction in number of Whig ladies of the royal household, and, on being rebuffed by the Queen, he refused to form a government.

In the election of November 1834, Peel addressed the people of his constituency, Tamworth, on issues of policy, this address becoming known as the Tamworth Manifesto – the first ever political manifesto, though unlike those of modern times. Peel became Prime Minister following this election, but his minority government lasted only six months. He returned as Prime Minister from 1841 to 1846, leading a strong government. He was an excellent orator and debater in the House. As a supporter of Free Trade, he repealed the Corn Laws in 1846; he reformed the Navigation Acts, which ruled, for instance, that imports should be carried on English ships; he reinstated income, at tax seven pence in the pound; and he carried out tariff reform, abolishing export taxes and greatly reducing the number and level of import duties on raw materials. He also worked for the reform of the electoral system, the Church and local government. The 1842 Coal Mines Act prohibited women and boys under ten years old from being employed down coal mines, while the 1844 Factory Act reduced the working day for women and children in factories to twelve hours and six-and-a-half hours, respectively. In foreign policy he worked for peace in Europe, China, India and Afghanistan. In 1846, Peel was defeated in the House on his Irish policy and resigned as Prime Minister, on the same day that the Corn Laws were repealed. Sir Robert Peel died in a riding accident in London in 1850 and is commemorated in a stone tower on Holcombe (Harcles) Hill, high above Ramsbottom.

John Bright (1811-1889) was born in Rochdale. He was a founder of the Anti-Corn Law League, and, with his friend and colleague Richard Cobden, led the League to success. He was a Member of Parliament for Durham and Manchester and became one of Parliament's greatest orators. He favoured Free Trade, extension of the franchise, disestablishment of Church of Ireland, reduced public spending and greater religious freedom. He was a Quaker, the first Nonconformist in the Cabinet, and worked for peace. He did not support the decision to go to war in the Crimea (1854-1856) and resigned from the Cabinet when Gladstone's policy in Egypt led to the bombardment of Alexandria in 1882. However, he supported the Union, the North, in the American Civil War. John Bright is buried in Rochdale.

Richard Assheton Cross (1823-1914) was born in Preston and served as Conservative Member of Parliament for Preston, South West Lancashire and Newton. He was Home Secretary in Disraeli's Government in the 1870s and in Lord Salisbury's Government in the 1880s he was Secretary for India and Chancellor of the Duchy of Lancaster. He played an important role in bringing about social reforms, introducing a Licensing Act, educational reforms and housing legislation, including slum clearance provisions. He was also prominent in reducing the severity of laws against trade unions. He was ennobled, becoming Viscount Cross of Broughton-in-Furness.

Edward Stanley, Fourteenth Earl of Derby (1799-1869), of Knowsley in Lancashire, served as Irish Secretary and Colonial Office under Earl Grey, playing a role in the abolition of slavery in the Colonies. He was in favour of the Corn Laws but served in Sir Robert Peel's 1841-1846 Conservative government which repealed them, and became Prime Minister himself in 1852, leading a weak government whose rising star was Benjamin Disraeli. The second Derby government of 1858 was also weak. It again included Disraeli. Derby's son, Lord Stanley, also served in this government, which was defeated on electoral reform. Derby served a third term as Prime Minister in 1866-1868, and during this government the 1867 Reform Act doubled the electorate, mainly in towns, and redistributed constituencies more fairly. Derby labelled this act 'a leap in the dark.' He finally resigned in 1868 and was succeeded in office by Disraeli. Derby's son, Edward Stanley, 15th Earl of Derby (1826-1893), served as Foreign Minister in Disraeli's 1874 Conservative government and was at the Colonial Office in Gladstone's government in 1880.

William Ewart Gladstone (1809-1898) was born and brought up in Liverpool, of Scottish extraction. He served as Home Secretary and four times as Chancellor of the Exchequer, one of the greatest Chancellors Britain has produced. He was also four times Prime Minister between 1868 and 1894. He represented Newark, Oxford University, South Lancashire, Greenwich and Midlothian in the House of Commons and served under Sir Robert Peel, working for repeal of Corn Laws and electoral reform. Gladstone's social policies were based on the belief that people should be allowed and encouraged to take responsibility for their own wellbeing. He was sympathetic towards the working man and considered it shameful that many working men and women were obliged to enter the workhouse in old age after a lifetime of hard labour. Over a long period, even when Prime Minister, he found time to minister to London's prostitutes. He entered Parliament as a Conservative, but disagreed with Conservative opposition to the repeal of the

Corn Laws. As a result, he and Sir Robert Peel joined the Liberals. Gladstone served under Lord Palmerston before becoming Prime Minister himself. Queen Victoria never got on with Prime Minister Gladstone. He worked for peace, low public expenditure, electoral reform and Home Rule for Ireland. In his quest to secure Home Rule for Ireland he was unsuccessful, thwarted by the House of Lords. He showed his Conservative colours by opposing the abolition of slavery and the passing of the Factory Acts. With Sir Robert Peel he reduced and simplified tariffs and duties, in the name of Free Trade, and reintroduced income tax, using it to pay for the Crimean War. He was responsible for the disestablishment of the Church of Ireland, army reform, Civil Service reform and the Licensing Act. His 1884 Reform Act added millions of voters to the electoral registers. Later in his political life, Gladstone was critical of the Second Afghan War and the Zulu War, but he oversaw the invasion of Egypt in 1882 and the dispatch of military expeditions into Sudan, which led to the death of General Gordon at Khartoum in 1884. As a result of the Gordon affair, Gladstone lost popularity and was criticised by the Queen. He resigned as Prime Minister in 1885. William Gladstone died in 1898 and is buried in Westminster Abbey

Lancashire can be proud of the contribution made by its politicians.

MANCHESTER AND THE 1832 REFORM ACT

At the close of the eighteenth century, Manchester was unrepresented in Parliament, whereas 100 boroughs having a cumulative population less than that of Manchester returned 200 members. Some rotten boroughs – such as Old Sarum in Wiltshire, with hardly any voters – sent members to Parliament. Clitheroe, with sixty burgesses, and Newton-le-Willows, with thirty-six, each elected two Members, whereas Manchester elected none. The population of Lancashire almost doubled between 1801 and 1831 and Manchester was prominent in the quest for recognition in terms of voting rights.

In 1792, liberal elements in the city founded the Manchester Constitutional Society, whose main aim was the encouragement of reform of the corrupt House of Commons. The Government reacted by encouraging local magistrates to take action against sedition and warning publicans that their licenses would be revoked if they allowed seditious meetings in their hostelries. There was a significant reaction among the populous against the agitation for liberal reforms. The liberals were branded Jacobins, and 186 publicans banned them from their premises. Drunken gangs were encouraged by the authorities to attack the homes of Jacobins, and the premises of the *Manchester Herald*, a newspaper set up by the liberals, were sacked. The leader of the reformers, Thomas Walker, defended his own house with firearms, and was tried in Lancaster for waging war against the King, but the case was dismissed due to the unreliability of the main witness.

As the Napoleonic Wars got underway, the Government used the emergency to stifle protest meetings. In retaliation, in 1796, the Manchester Thinking Club was established, its members meeting in groups of up to 300, remaining silent during such meetings, and wearing muzzles with the word 'MUM' written across them. They substituted thought for debate!

The plight of the workers deteriorated as the war progressed. A meeting of weavers in May 1808, calling for minimum rates of pay, was dispersed by the militia, following the reading of the Riot Act, and a weaver was killed during the action. In April 1812, a town meeting called by anti-reformers was hijacked by the reformers and some damage was done to the Exchange by rioters. Further food riots and machine-breaking took place over subsequent weeks. The authorities used spies to encourage acts of sedition and then to betray the perpetrators.

In 1815, a group of reformers led by John Knight met in the Prince Regent's Arms, Ancoats, in order to petition

Parliament for peace and Parliamentary reform. The meeting was broken up the military, led by Jo Nadin, the constable, blunderbuss in hand. Thirty-seven reformers were arrested and sent by the notoriously biased magistrate, the Revd W.R. Hay, for trial at Lancaster. Nadin had used a spy, Fletcher, who declared that he had asked to be sworn in as a member of a seditious society. The reformers were therefore all accused of administering illegal oaths, and were not allowed to testify in each other's favour. However, one of the reformers present at the meeting had not been apprehended, and he testified that no oaths were administered and that the two reformers who had been accused of administering the oath were not, in fact, present at the time. The case was dismissed. In 1816, a group of reformers met at St Peter's Fields in Manchester and decided to walk to London to petition against reduced freedoms and in favour of annual Parliaments and universal suffrage. They were called the Blanketeers, since they each carried a blanket to provide a little warmth at night. The meeting was dispersed by the military and those who managed to set off for London were apprehended en route. Many were arrested, including Samuel Bamford, the weaver-poet. Following the examination of some in London by the Secretary of State, all cases were dismissed.

In June 1819, reformers meeting at St Peter's Fields decided to embarrass the Government by promulgating an embargo on products such as coffee, tea and spirits which earned significant tax income. A meeting was called to elect a legislative representative for Manchester, since no Members could be elected to Parliament. The meeting was declared illegal and banned. A town meeting was requested and the request refused, so the reformers planned a huge open-air meeting in St Peter's Fields for 16 August 1819. 80,000 people attended, from Rochdale, Middleton, Ashton, Oldham, Stockport, and so on, including women and the elderly, in holiday spirit and Sunday clothing. Some had been drilled to teach them how to march in orderly fashion, and this was taken by the authorities to indicate that the gathering was military in nature.

Henry 'Orator' Hunt was the main speaker, but, as he started to speak, Mr H.H. Birley sent the mounted Manchester Yeomanry into the crowd, swords drawn, slashing as they went. The 15th Hussars then galloped in, using the flat rather than the edge of their swords. The outcome of this peaceful assembly was ten men and one woman dead and 600 injured. The Revd W.R. Hay was the architect of the Peterloo Massacre. He may have read the Riot Act from a window, at which peaceable citizens ought to have withdrawn, but, if he did, no one heard him. England was appalled, as truthful accounts were written in the London papers. Even a *Times* correspondent had been arrested by Jo Nadin as a conspirator, underlining the dishonesty of those who sought to justify the action. The middle and working classes of Manchester were united in their condemnation. Even the cabinet was appalled, but had to back the authorities as they needed to be seen to defend law and order.

Of those reformers who were arrested, Hunt was jailed for two years, and Bamford and three others received a one-year sentence. Court actions were taken against the assailants, but none succeeded. Mr Hay moved to Rochdale Parish, where he spent the rest of his life ignominiously.

In 1830, with the death of George IV, and with a successful revolution in France leading to reform there, the pace of reform quickened. The Duke of Wellington, Prime Minister, opposed reform but was replaced by Earl Grey who was committed to it. There was an election in 1831 and the blocking Tories lost, the people preferring reform to the threat of revolution. Reform Bills were introduced in 1831, the newly elected Orator Hunt playing his part in the debates, but were blocked by the Lords, leading to further protest meetings in Manchester and riots elsewhere in the country. The Reform Bill passed by the Commons in December 1831 was threatened with rejection by the Lords, the King refusing to allow Earl Grey to create liberal Lords to outvote the Tories. Earl Grey resigned and was replaced by the Duke of Wellington, whose opinion was that the voting system was not broken and did not need fixing. Manchester was incensed.

Its Reform Committee, meeting daily, sent a petition of 24,000 signatures to London, seeking the cessation of supplies (funding) unless the Lords relented. It had a grand send-off and was fêted in cities that it passed through. There were further meetings at Peterloo, Salford, Chorlton and around the country. The outcry forced the King to recall Earl Grey and the Reform Bill passed into law on 7 June 1832, with the Lords abstaining on a large scale.

The 1832 Reform Act eradicated rotten boroughs and increased the British electorate from 435,000 to 685,000 – out of a population of 16.5 million. However, this, of course, was only the beginning. In 1832, Lancashire elected only fourteen MPs, two for the County and two each for the towns of Liverpool, Preston, Lancaster, Wigan, Newton and Clitheroe. The 1832 Act allocated twenty-four seats in Parliament to Lancashire, comprising two for the County, two each for the towns of Manchester, Blackburn, Bolton, Oldham, Liverpool, Preston, Lancaster and Wigan, and one each for Salford, Burnley, Rochdale, Ashton, Warrington and Clitheroe. Chartists and others agitated for further reforms and the 1867 Act gave the vote to all male householders and renters of houses. Lancashire was awarded thirty-three seats and this was increased to fifty-six seats in 1884, one-twelfth of the entire House of Commons membership.

But women did not yet have the vote, and in 1903 Emmeline Pankhurst and her daughters, Christabel and Sylvia, founded the Women's Social and Political Union in Manchester to press for female suffrage. In 1906, Christabel and another young woman, Annie Kenny, interrupted a meeting in the Free Trade Hall addressed by Sir Edward Grey and attended by Winston Churchill (Member of Parliament for Oldham and, later, North-west Manchester). The ladies were fined, and then jailed for non-payment of the fines. The long process of electoral reform was not substantially completed until women were given the vote on the same terms as men in 1928. Manchester can be well pleased with the part it played in the reform process.

THE REPEAL OF THE CORN LAWS

Lancashire played a significant role in the repeal of the Corn Laws. These laws of 1815 were intended to help British farmers by keeping the price of corn high. They achieved this by banning imports of corn unless the price rose above a certain high level. Cheap imports were therefore not allowed to compete with home-grown corn, and the British people felt the effect, in high food prices. The populace complained bitterly, leading to the founding of the Anti-Corn Law League in the York Hotel, Manchester, in 1838. Richard Cobden, who came from Sussex but had a calico-manufacturing business in Manchester, and John Bright, the Rochdale carpet manufacturer, were leading lights in the League, and in 1841, Prime Minister Robert Peel was persuaded to reverse his support for the Corn Laws, which were repealed in 1846. The result was cheaper food, together with cheaper raw materials as the benefits of Free Trade spread. Manchester's role in the repeal of the Corn Laws was marked with the building of its fine Free Trade Hall in 1856, on the site of its brick predecessor, which itself replaced the original wooden structure built in 1840. Lancashire celebrated with a public holiday and there seemed to be some truth in the saying that what Manchester thinks today London will think tomorrow.

In 1844, a group of mill-workers in Rochdale, unhappy at high food prices, decided to take matters into their own hands. They formed the Rochdale Society of Equitable Pioneers, owned by its customers and cutting out the middleman. Their first premises were in Toad Lane. The enterprise flourished and from such humble beginnings what we now know as the Cooperative Society emerged.

LITERARY LANCASHIRE IN THE NINETEENTH CENTURY

Although not of Lancastrian origin, Mrs Gaskell is worthy of mention in any book about Lancashire. She was born

Elizabeth Cleghorn Stevenson in London in September 1810. Her father was a native of Berwick-upon-Tweed. Her mother, a Holland, was from Knutsford in Cheshire, and died shortly after Elizabeth's birth, so Elizabeth was brought up by the Holland family in Knutsford. After completion of her schooling in Warwickshire she lived at Knutsford, but spent some time with Holland relatives in London. She also visited Newcastle upon Tyne and stayed with a Unitarian minister, a distant relative, whose daughter was married to the minister of Cross Street Unitarian Chapel in Manchester. Through him, Elizabeth met William Gaskell from Warrington, the assistant minister at Cross Street. The two were married in Knutsford Parish Church in 1832, and, thereafter, Elizabeth preferred to be known as Mrs Gaskell.

Mrs Gaskell wrote the novels *Cranford, Mary Barton, Cousin Phyllis, Ruth, North and South,* and *Wives and Daughters.* In her novels she demonstrated her knowledge of industry and the plight of industrial workers. Mrs Gaskell's retreat, where she apparently did some writing, was Lindeth Tower, at Silverdale, overlooking Morecambe Bay. The Gaskell Memorial Hall in Silverdale marks her links with the town. The name 'Cranford' is probably derived from the 'Cran' in Cranage, a village a few miles south of Knutsford, and the 'ford' in Knutsford itself.

Perhaps Mrs Gaskell's most important work was *The Life of Charlotte Brontë,* published in 1857. Mrs Gaskell was introduced to Charlotte Brontë in 1850 by the Kay-Shuttleworth's (of Gawthorpe Hall, Padiham) at their house at Briery Close, near Windermere. Charlotte visited the Gaskells at Plymouth Grove, Manchester, in 1854, apparently while in Manchester shopping for her wedding trousseau. Charlotte only met Mrs Gaskell a few times, but they were close enough for Mrs Gaskell to call her 'my dear friend' in her biography.

Charlotte Brontë died on 31 March 1855. She had been married for nine months and was pregnant. In June 1855, Ellen Nussey, Charlotte's friend since schooldays, prompted Patrick Brontë, father of the Brontë sisters, to invite

Mrs Gaskell to write a biography of Charlotte, a project that Mrs Gaskell already had in mind. Ellen Nussey and Patrick Brontë were motivated by the need to correct erroneous reports that had appeared in obituary notices. It may be that they wanted to establish a sanitised version of Charlotte's life to counter the stories that were circulating about her, which may have contained some truth. Charles Dickens refused to publish one such story in *Household Words*, the magazine of which he was editor, in deference to the sensibilities of Charlotte's bereaved father and husband.

Mrs Gaskell died suddenly in 1865 at The Lawn, in Alton, Hampshire, a few days after taking possession of the property that she secretly bought for her husband's retirement.

The Brontë sisters, of whom Mrs Gaskell wrote, lived a few miles over the East Lancashire-Yorkshire border, at the Parsonage, Haworth. Lancashire played a sombre role in the lives of the Brontës. According to Charlotte's biographer, Mrs Gaskell, a walk in a damp meadow whilst visiting Gawthorpe Hall, Padiham, in early 1855 worsened Charlotte's already weak medical condition. Charlotte died in March 1855. It also has to be admitted that Lancashire was involved in other Brontë tragedies. In 1824, Maria, Elizabeth, Charlotte and Emily Brontë were sent to the Clergy Daughters' School at Cowan Bridge, in north Lancashire, close to Kirkby Lonsdale. Conditions at the school were awful, and the girls suffered much. In 1825, both Maria and Elizabeth died from consumption, and Charlotte and Emily were withdrawn from the school. The sisters' sufferings at Cowan Bridge school were immortalised in the depiction of Lowood House school in Charlotte's *Jane Eyre*.

There is anecdotal evidence that Charlotte, together with one or more of her sisters, visited the Lancashire village of Wycoller, 8 miles or so from Haworth, and local folklore has it that the ruined Wycoller Hall was the template for Ferndean Manor, where Jane Eyre renewed her acquaintance with Mr Rochester. Charlotte Brontë ventured further down the Lancashire Calder Valley, visiting Sir James and Lady Kay-Shuttleworth at Gawthorpe Hall, Padiham, on two occasions. On one such occasion the Kay-Shuttleworths took Charlotte to Whalley Abbey and Mitton Hall. On two occasions the Kay-Shuttleworths visited the Brontë Parsonage at Haworth. Charlotte married the Revd Arthur Bell Nicholls in 1854, and the Revd Nicholls was offered a living at All Saints Church, close to Gawthorpe Hall, but he turned down the offer, to remain at Haworth as Charlotte needed to look after her father.

Charles Dickens visited Lancashire many times during his reading and acting tours. He attended several charity and educational soirees in Manchester and Liverpool and sailed twice to the United States from Liverpool. He made Liverpool his unofficial headquarters in the north-west and also visited Lancaster, Preston, Blackburn, Blackpool and Bolton. His sister lived in Manchester. He met Sir James Kay-Shuttleworth but did not accept Sir James' invitation to visit Gawthorpe Hall. Dickens also met Mrs Gaskell, visited her in Manchester and serialised *North and South* in Household Words. He seems to have used Preston as a model for Coketown in *Hard Times* and he conceived the idea for *A Christmas Carol* whilst staying in Manchester. From the same city, in the words of his friend John Forster, he 'brought away his Brothers Cheeryble', the Cheerybles in *The Life and Adventures of Nicholas Nickleby* being based upon the Grant Brothers, who Dickens met through the auspices of Lancashire novelist Harrison Ainsworth. Dickens was in Lancashire looking for background for his novels. He later said that he had visited the worst cotton mill and the best, but there was no great difference between them!

Whilst visiting Preston in 1867, Charles Dickens managed to link himself with one of Lancashire's favourite legends, the knighting of the loin of beef by King James I in 1617. On 25 April, Dickens and his readings manager, George Dolby, walked along the old road from Preston to Blackburn, and came across Hoghton Tower, then in decay and used as a farmhouse. Dolby later wrote that 'Having some knowledge of the history of the place, Mr Dickens decided on making an inspection.' It appears that Dickens knew of the existence of the Tower. Given Dickens' friendship with Harrison Ainsworth, one might be forgiven for suspecting that Ainsworth had told Dickens about the Tower, years earlier, or, more probably, that Dickens had read Ainsworth's *The Lancashire Witches* (1848), in which Hoghton Tower features prominently and which would have encouraged him to visit the Tower, when in the vicinity. Whatever the case, the resident farmer allowed them to look round the old Tower and Dickens' impressions of the place are recorded in, and had a significant influence on, his short story, the semi-auto-biographical *George Silverman's Explanation* (1868).

There are some similarities between Dickens' description of Hoghton Tower in *George Silverman's Explanation* and Ainsworth's description in *The Lancashire Witches*, as if Dickens was borrowing details from *The Lancashire Witches*. In his description of the Tower and its setting, Ainsworth refers to two rivers, the Ribble and the Darwen. Dickens mentions the same two rivers, 'the Rivers Ribble and Darwen glancing below', although the Ribble can hardly be said to glance below the Tower, being several miles to the north.

Dickens mentions two views, 'two distances', both smoky ones, probably in the direction of Preston and Blackburn. He seems to be purposely contrasting his two nineteenth-century industrial views with those rural and pleasing views in two directions that King James had when, according to Ainsworth, he looked from his window, towards 'on the one hand, the vast forest of Myerscough and Bowland' in the north, 'and, on the other, an open but still undulating country' towards Preston and the sea in the north-west.

Next, and most importantly, Dickens uses information from *The Lancashire Witches* when he describes the Tower as: 'A house, centuries old, on high ground a mile or so removed from the road between Preston and Blackburn, where the first James of England, in his hurry to make money by making baronets, perhaps made some of those remunerative dignitaries.' Closer scrutiny reveals a cryptic message hidden in Dickens' words. When he says that James 'made', i.e. 'knighted', 'some of those remunerative dignitaries', he meant part of a ruminative dignitary, not a remunerative one. A play on words by Dickens may be suspected here. And what particular part of a ruminative dignitary? Why, the loin, of course! Thus, the knighting of 'some of those remunerative dignitaries' becomes the knighting of the loin of beef to create sirloin, just as had been related in *The Lancashire Witches*.

As a final piece of evidence, it can be seen that Dickens' use of the word 'dignitaries' reflects King James' declaration in *The Lancashire Witches* that the loin of beef should have some 'dignity': '"A loin!" exclaimed James, taking the carving-knife from the sewer, who stood by. "By my faith that is not title honourable enough for joint sae worthy. It wants a dignity, and it shall hae it. Henceforth," he added, touching the meat with the flat of the long blade, as if placing the sword on the back of a knight expectant, "henceforth, it shall be SIR-LOIN, an' see ye ca' it sae."'

Interestingly, as Peter Ackroyd points out, Dickens wrote that he had experienced 'the strangest impression of reality and originality... I feel as if I had read something (by somebody else) which I should never get out of my head!!' Although there is no doubt that Dickens was here talking about the inspiration that he gained for his approach to the story, this reference to 'something' written by 'somebody else' could just as well be applied to The Lancashire Witches written by Harrison Ainsworth. It may be that Dickens made this cryptic reference to Ainsworth's knighting of the loin because he felt some remorse at having parted company with Ainsworth as a close friend many years previously. Perhaps he was here making a gesture of acknowledgment towards Ainsworth, for old time's sake. Ainsworth and Lancashire seem to have influenced Charles Dickens in some little way in the writing of this tale. Whatever the case, the revelation of a link between Charles Dickens and the knighting of the loin is particularly timely, coinciding with the recent 900th anniversary of Hoghton Tower and the bicentenary of Dickens' birth in 2012.

William Harrison Ainsworth was born in King Street, Manchester, on 4 February 1805. He trained as a solicitor, but the profession was not to his liking. He preferred writing as a career. His popular novels were historical in nature, based on fact but with a liberal helping of fiction and the supernatural. Several of his novels addressed aspects of Lancashire history, including the aforementioned *Lancashire Witches*, *The Manchester Rebels*, *Preston Fight*, *Mervyn Clitheroe* and *The Leaguers of Lathom*. His tendency to mix fact and fiction led many of his readers to confuse the two. Thus, some of his fictitious tales were accepted as fact and entered into folklore. The best examples are Dick Turpin's twenty-four-hour ride from London to York in on his faithful steed, Black Bess, in *Rookwood* and, as mentioned, the knighting of the loin of beef at Hoghton Tower.

Ainsworth was a particularly good friend of Charles Dickens, and was godfather to his son, Henry Fielding Dickens. Their first meeting may have been in the offices of *The Morning Chronicle* in 1834 or 1835. They corresponded often and met several times, including one occasion in 1838 when Dickens, his illustrator Hablot Knight Browne and John Forster visited Manchester. Ainsworth introduced Dickens to John Forster and his own publisher and friend John Macrone, and it was Macrone who published Dickens' first successful work, *Sketches by Boz*. Ainsworth also introduced Dickens to others in his literary circle, such as William Makepiece Thackeray, and had a hand in Dickens' teaming up with George Cruikshank as an illustrator. The literati of the day attended frequent literary gatherings and dinners at Ainsworth's Kensal Lodge home in west London. Dickens, Ainsworth, Thackeray, Cruikshank and others formed the Fraserians, a literary grouping named after, and meeting in the premises of, *Fraser's Magazine*.

Dickens was impressed by the older Ainsworth and aspired to emulate his success, fame and beau-like stylishness. He introduced into his early works some of the romantic, adventurous literary style that was a feature of Ainsworth's own successful novels. In December 1838,

Dickens, Forster and Ainsworth formed the Trio Club, a close circle of friends. The three of them commonly rode out together and dined together regularly. Ainsworth, among others, attended a dinner at Greenwich to welcome Dickens home (via Liverpool) from the USA. On another occasion, a dinner was arranged by the worthies of Manchester in honour of Ainsworth, and Ainsworth invited Dickens to join him for companionship. Not surprisingly, Dickens stole the limelight, not through his own fault, but Ainsworth was magnanimous about the incident and showed no resentment towards Dickens.

Dickens proposed Ainsworth as his replacement as editor of *Bentley's Miscellany* magazine, and the proprietor, George Bentley, agreed, albeit reluctantly. In his letter of farewell, published in the magazine, Dickens described the new editor, Ainsworth, as 'one of my most intimate and valued friends.' At this point (March-April, 1839), the Dickens-Ainsworth friendship came under strain, for one or more of several reasons. It is only natural that a degree of competitiveness existed between the two writers. Ainsworth was the first to succeed, with *Rookwood* in 1834, which brought him almost overnight fame. Dickens followed with *Pickwick* in 1836, *Oliver Twist* in 1837 and *Nicholas Nickleby* in 1839. Ainsworth's novel *Jack Sheppard*, 1839, was a huge success and out-sold *Oliver Twist* for a time, but subsequently Dickens' fame and fortune accelerated, leaving Ainsworth behind in his wake.

A second factor in the cooling of relations between the writers revolved around an incident in 1839. Dickens was reaching the height of his fame, but was locked into a contract with *Bentley's Miscellany* that earned him hardly enough, in his opinion, to support his family, the contract being signed before Dickens achieved great fame. He felt that he was exploited and that he was being paid significantly below his market value. Consequently, he wanted to abandon the writing of *Barnaby Rudge* and concentrate on more remunerative work. Dickens' and Ainsworth's mutual friend, John Forster, persuaded Dickens to merely postpone *Barnaby Rudge* for six months, and alerted Richard Bentley (brother of George) to Dickens' concerns. Bentley blamed Forster, wrongly, for inciting Dickens to break his agreement, and Bentley's claims circulated among their friends and business acquaintances, to Forster's detriment. Bentley seems to have quoted Ainsworth as being in sympathy with his own views on the issue, since Ainsworth had been in Bentley's presence when those views were expounded and had done nothing to correct or refute them.

Dickens felt that Ainsworth had not defended Forster from allegations of disloyalty, and told him so by letter. Dickens asked Ainsworth to write to Bentley, informing him that Forster was not to blame for the problems between Dickens and Bentley. Presumably, Ainsworth did this, possibly by word of mouth, as he elicited a letter from Bentley, absolving himself (Ainsworth) of responsibility for Forster's role in the Bentley-Dickens dispute. This seems to have resolved the issue, but, although they remained friends and continued to correspond and meet occasionally, it seems that Dickens doubted the steadfastness of Ainsworth's friendship. The Dickens-Ainsworth friendship was never quite the same again and Ainsworth ceased to be a member of the Trio Club in 1839.

Finally, the 'Newgate controversy' damaged Harrison Ainsworth's reputation and can not have failed to drive a wedge into the Dickens-Ainsworth relationship. The controversy arose in 1839, when Ainsworth and other novelists were criticised for the violence portrayed in their 'axe-in-the-neck', gothic style novels and for glorifying crime and criminals such as Jack Sheppard and Dick Turpin. Following the Newgate controversy and his eclipse by Dickens, Ainsworth concentrated on historical dramas, with detailed descriptions of ancient edifices, as in *Guy Fawkes*, *The Tower of London*, *Old St Pauls* and *Windsor Castle*. Nicholas Rance described his works as an 'incongruous merging of historical romance and guide book', while Stephen Carver comments that 'Ainsworth's creative vision was an idiosyncratic one, and ... he was punished by the literary establishment as a result, assisted, indirectly, by his

own refusal to conform to the moral and aesthetic stand-
ards of the Victorian novel.' In his preface to *Rookwood*,
Ainsworth himself admitted that he had 'an eye rather to the
reader's amusement than his edification'. Carver describes
him as aiming his works at the rabble.

Thus, Ainsworth's style did not evolve, he was increasingly
ignored by academics and he faded from view as a national
literary celebrity, his work becoming merely 'provincial melo-
drama'. However, and not surprisingly, Ainsworth continued
to have a huge following in Lancashire and was ultimately
rewarded with the title 'The Lancashire Novelist'. His last
major work, and his most enduring one, was *The Lancashire
Witches* of 1848, the first of his Lancashire Novels, serialised
in his own *Ainsworth's Magazine*. Ainsworth's last recorded
meeting with Dickens was in London in June 1854. He was
shocked by Dickens' death in 1870 and regretted not meeting
up with him in their later years, for old times' sake.

In later life, Ainsworth was fêted in Manchester, as befits
the celebrity he was. In October 1879, he attended a dinner
given in his honour by his old school, Manchester Grammar
School. There followed a more-distinguished occasion, a
banquet in September 1881, given in Ainsworth's honour by
the Lord Mayor of Manchester in recognition of his services
to literature and the high esteem in which he was held as a
citizen of Manchester. The banquet was a triumphant affair
and Ainsworth was greatly moved, as a proud Mancunian
and proud Lancastrian. In his speech acknowledging the
honours bestowed upon him, Ainsworth told his audience
that: 'My desire has really been to write a Lancashire novel,
a novel that should please the whole county, and I don't care
whether it pleased anyone else.'

Harrison Ainsworth died in 1882 and is buried at Kensal
Green Cemetery, West London. Ainsworth's influence on
Dickens character, career and works was a lasting legacy and
a tribute to Lancashire. Portraits of Ainsworth and Dickens
by Daniel Maclise grace the early editions of Ainsworth's and
Dickens' works, respectively, and a portrait of Ainsworth,
by Maclise, hangs in the Walker Art Gallery in Liverpool.

CHAPTER SEVEN

THE COTTON INDUSTRY AND ITS INVENTORS

GENERAL HISTORY OF COTTON

This subject is of particular interest to me, since I spent several college holidays in the 1960s working in cotton mills to supplement my student grant. At Portsmouth College of Technology in the 1960s, Dr Riley expounded the view that the cotton industry flourished in upland Lancashire because the region was unsuitable for other kinds of economic activity. Certainly, many other factors played their part, as traditionally recorded. The area was damp, which made for stronger yarn with fewer breakages. There was ample soft water for textile manufacturing processes, such as washing, bleaching and dying. There was ample water to power the mills during the first stage of the Industrial Revolution and ample coal to power the steam engines of the next stage. Chemicals for bleaching and dying were available close by, as in the salt deposits of Cheshire and the coalfields of Lancashire. Wool was a staple of the region, an important factor given that the early Lancashire textile industry was dominated by woollens, and there was a growing labour force to spin and weave it. But it is in the nature of human beings to seek to improve their lot in life, and the possibilities in upland Lancashire were severely limited.

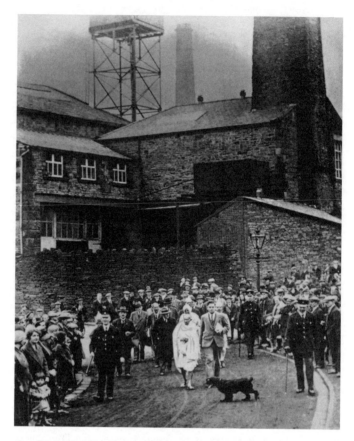

Gandhi visiting a Darwen textile factory in 1931.

The climate, terrain and soil conditions militated against significant expansion of arable output, and they were far from the sea, so they could not supplement their diets by fishing. Nor could they benefit from sea-trade. If they were to better their lot, what else was there for them to do but exploit the skills and resources that were available to them, and turn a domestic activity, based on self-subsistence, into a wealth-creating industry? The initial impetus, then, was necessity.

Lancashire was already sending fustians (a mixture of linen and coarse cotton) to the London market in the seventeenth century, but in the early eighteenth century, the textile industry was dominated by woollen cloth manufacture, and almost all the textiles made in Lancashire were woollen in nature. The wool lobby was powerful in Parliament, and, when the East India Co. started to import printed and dyed calicoes (cloths made entirely from cotton) from Hindustan, the woollen manufacturers managed to have an Act passed, in 1700, banning such imports. This was followed by a ban on the import of plain Indian calicoes that could be printed or dyed in England. Lancashire started to produce its own heavier equivalent of calicoes, fustians (fustian is derived from Fostat, near Cairo, the area that originally produced them), having linen warp for the loom and cotton weft for the primitive shuttle, but this activity was banned in 1721. Even the wearing of printed or dyed calicoes or equivalents was illegal. The woollen manufacturers were protecting themselves from competing fabrics.

In 1736, the cotton manufacturers of Lancashire persuaded Parliament to pass the 'Manchester Act' which permitted the manufacture and printing or dying of cloth with linen warp and cotton weft (fustians), whilst retaining high duties on Indian imports. The linen warp came mainly from Northern Ireland. Protected, as it was, from Indian imports, the Lancashire cotton industry expanded rapidly, as evidenced by the increase in imports of raw cotton from 1,545,000 pounds weight in 1730 to 3,870,000 pounds in 1764. Initially, it was usual for merchants to issue raw cotton and linen warp to the domestic artisan, who, with his family and perhaps a helper or two, would spin the raw cotton into yarn, to be used as the weft, and then weave the cloth, returning it to the merchant who would travel around selling to shopkeepers or whoever would buy it. In the mid-eighteenth century it became more common for a middleman to farm out the materials to the artisans, collect the cloth and sell it in Manchester to merchants who would finish it, print or dye it and distribute it around the nation and abroad. Raw cotton, yarn and cloth were carried on packhorses, at that time.

Typically, some spinning and weaving was done by cottagers, working full-time, but much textile work was done on farms, otherwise engaged in producing oats, potatoes, milk, butter and cheese. Farm work came first, then, in the family's spare time, the preparation of the materials, the spinning and the weaving processes were performed. In the late eighteenth century the typical farm would have four looms. Women and children would do the preparation and spinning, men the weaving. The value of the spinning and the weaving to the family might or might not exceed the value of the farm products they produced. But the spinners could not keep pace with the weavers, especially at harvest times when effort was diverted into farming. Before the flying-shuttle came into operation, one handloom weaver consumed the yarn produced by three spinners, using single-spindle traditional spinning machines. The shortage of yarn was a big problem, and the supply situation was aggravated by the invention of Kay's flying-shuttle, following which six or eight spinners were needed to supply one weaver. Thus, John Kay's invention stimulated equivalent inventions in the spinning industry, without which the Lancashire cotton industry would have been unable to expand.

The sum effect of all these inventions was the almost total movement away from the manufacture of woollens and fustians in Lancashire, and the concentration on cotton, leading to the rapid expansion of the cotton industry and the establishment of the world's first industrial society. Improvements in other processes complemented the benefits of Lancashire's inventiveness. In the eighteenth century, finished cloth was laid out in the fields, to be bleached by sunlight, a painfully slow process. Towards the end of the century, chemical bleaching took over, a much faster process. The dying process was also greatly improved and accelerated in the mid-nineteenth century, with the discovery of artificial dyes extracted from coal tar. The yarn could be dyed to create patterns on the cloth, or the whole cloth piece could be dyed in a uniform colour. The printing of patterns onto calicoes was a process that had been developing since late eighteenth century, and printing technology kept pace with spinning and weaving improvements. Incidentally, the manufacture of cloth in pieces gave rise to the expression 'piece-work' that became common throughout the industry.

By the end of the eighteenth century, the improvements in spinning had created a surplus of thread, and a further break-through in weaving was required. A Leicestershire parson, Edmund Cartwright, patented a power loom in 1785, but initially it was hardly faster than the handloom, although five weavers could run six looms. The original power-loom was difficult to operate. Cartwright built a weaving shed in Doncaster in 1787, driven initially by bulls but by steam within two years. However, the venture failed in 1793. Even by 1830 the power-loom had not been perfected, but gradual improvements led to the widespread use of the Lancashire loom by 1850, and it was considered to be the world's best. Each weaver was able to run two power-looms, driven by steam power, but even in 1850 there were still some hand-loom weavers operating in the county.

Another factor that played an important part in the rapid expansion of the Lancashire cotton industry was the ever-increasing supply of raw cotton from the United States at ever-lower prices. There was great pressure on supplies from the West Indies and eastern producers, which formed the bulk of supplies until the 1790s, but at that point these traditional sources were outstripped by supplies from the southern states of the USA, the slave states. Raw cotton from the USA was clean, thanks to American Eli Whitney, who invented the saw gin in 1793, a machine that removed seeds and most of the other plant contaminants from the cotton boll. This was a great help to Lancashire, as cotton from other sources had to be cleaned before use. Some 3 million pounds weight of raw cotton were imported in 1760, rising to 5.3 millions in 1781, 32.5 millions in 1789 and some 50 million pounds per annum in the later Napoleonic period. Raw cotton became Britain's main import and remained so between 1825 and 1873.

Between 1766 and 1787, cotton cloth output increased more than five times. In 1787 there were forty cotton mills in

Lancashire and 119 in the whole of England, mostly powered
by water. By 1819 there were 344 cotton mills in Lancashire
and by 1839 the number had risen to 1,815. By 1800, steam
engines were used increasingly to power those mills, the first
being installed in Manchester in 1789 and another in Bolton
in 1790. Eighty-two Boulton and Watt steam engines were
delivered to Lancashire from Birmingham between 1785
and 1800. Cotton textile exports exceeded woollen exports
for the first time in 1803 and accounted for half of the country's exports by 1830, thanks to mechanisation and cheap
raw cotton which gave Lancashire an unbeatable competi-
tive advantage. India became Lancashire's main customer by
1831, despite the low cost of Indian labour. It was claimed
that Lancashire could meet the needs of the home market
before breakfast, devoting the rest of the day to exports.
Specialised textiles were also emerging, as in the case of
waterproofed clothing developed in Manchester by the Scot,
Charles Macintosh.

Queen Victoria and Prince Albert came to see the industrial colossus that was Lancashire in 1851, visiting Liverpool
and Manchester and sailing on the Bridgewater Canal at
Worsley. The Prince visited Dean Mills at Barrowbridge,
near Bolton, and gained first-hand experience of a no-doubt
sanitised cotton mill.

The development of the Lancashire cotton industry was
obviously not without pain. The plight of child labourers,
for instance, was a national disgrace. There were also many
periods of unrest, where workers felt threatened by new
inventions and where they resorted to mob violence to resist
the relentless march of progress. There were outbreaks of violence in 1753 when John Kay's house in Bury was attacked,
and in the late 1760s the mob attacked James Hargreaves'
house and Robert Peel's mill, destroying Spinning Jennies.
Hargreaves' Chorley factory was destroyed in 1779. Other
mills were damaged in the same disturbances, two rioters
killed and others detained and ultimately transported to
the Colonies. Bolton, Wigan and Blackburn were attacked,
but Sir George Saville and the Yorkshire militia, together

with local militia and armed army pensioners, deterred further violence in Preston, Chorley, Wigan and Blackburn. Handloom weavers burned a Manchester factory in 1790 and there were further attacks in 1812 and 1826. However, the loom-breakers were acting against the best interests of themselves and their descendants, and they failed to stem the march of progress.

Output peaked in 1912. In 1913 cotton textiles lost their place as Britain's most valuable export, being supplanted by machinery exports. By the First World War, cotton still accounted for a quarter of Britain's exports, falling to 16 per cent by 1930 and less than 10 per cent in the 1950s, at which point Britain became a net importer for the first time since the eighteenth century. Following a short-lived boom after the First World War, the industry went into several decades of decline. Since the middle of the nineteenth century, low-cost countries had been establishing and expanding their own cotton textile industries. Cotton was often the first industry to be established in developing countries as it was relatively easy to introduce and had a ready-made home market in each of those countries. Prior to 1843, the export of textile machinery was illegal, but such exports became legal in 1843 and these nascent overseas industries were supplied with machinery exported by Lancashire manufacturers. India, Brazil and Japan were prominent in building up their own industries. They first took less yarn from Britain, but thereafter took less cloth, and finally, having competed with Lancashire producers in their own internal markets, they began to compete with Lancashire in other countries. Britain lost most of its share of world trade in textiles between 1913 and 1939, and Japan became the world's biggest exporter of cotton textiles after 1933.

New producers tended to use newer machinery than that used by producers in Lancashire. They were organised differently. Whereas south Lancashire concentrated on spinning and North-east Lancashire on weaving, the spinning, weaving and finishing processes were brought together in the developing countries. Lancashire suffered from complacency, failing to replace its ageing looms with more modern machines. J.H. Northrop invented the automatic loom, incorporating a device that automatically replaced shuttles, whose weft had been used up, with full shuttles, without the necessity of having to stop the loom. Britain showed no interest in the machine, and it was patented in the USA in 1894. A more-efficient method of spinning termed 'ringspinning' was in use in the USA in the nineteenth century but was only introduced in Britain in the 1950s.

The Lancashire cotton industry suffered a severe setback in the 1920s when the Government of India imposed tariffs on imported cloth and Mahatma Gandhi called for a boycott of foreign cotton. These measures were, of course, intended to protect the rapidly developing Indian cotton industry. The blow fell hardest on the Blackburn-Darwen area, which depended most on the Indian market. Charles Nevin recounts that Gandhi visited England in 1931 for talks on the political future of India. Mr J.P. Davies, the Quaker owner of Greenfield Mill in Darwen, arranged for Gandhi to be invited to visit Darwen to witness the adverse effects of his boycott on the area's economy, presumably in the hope of persuading him to end his boycott. He stayed in Spring Vale Garden Village, Darwen, and was cordially received by dignitaries and a curious local populace. During consultations with industrialists and dignitaries, Gandhi expressed sorrow at the plight of Lancashire workers but said that the plight of his own countrymen was much worse, and he was unable to do anything to help Lancashire. India was merely following the path England had taken in developing industry in order to generate wealth. Lancashire should not hope for a return to the old trade and should diversify in order to improve its situation.

In the eighteenth century, Lancashire was one of India's main markets for textiles, and Gandhi reminded his hosts that, by developing its own textile industry, Lancashire had ruined the Indian industry. Lancashire could not complain now that the roles were reversed. In any case, closure of the Indian market was only part of Lancashire's problem. So, the pleas of the Lancashire textile industry came to naught.

During the twentieth century, oil-based man-made fibres provided further competition for the Lancashire cotton industry. In 1959, the Cotton Industry Act provided compensation to manufacturers who scrapped machinery. The effect was immediate, and in two years the Lancashire cotton textiles workforce was reduced by almost a third. Twelve million spindles and 105,000 looms were decommissioned and by the early 1980s most of Lancashire's cotton mills were closed. A few working steam-powered cotton mills are still in operation. The one at Queen Street Mill, Burnley, is open to the public as a museum piece. As an apprentice, my uncle, George Etherington, assisted in the refurbishment and installation of the mill's steam engine after the Second World War, the engine being appropriately named Peace.

The inventiveness of Lancastrians John Kay, James Hargreaves, Richard Arkwright and Samuel Crompton played an important role in the development of the Lancashire cotton industry. Their stories are recounted below.

JOHN KAY, 1704-1780

John Kay was born in Walmersby, near Bury, on 16 July 1704. Bury was a woollen-producing area, and Kay's father was involved in that trade. The family moved to Colchester, in Essex, where Kay's father became the owner of a woollen mill, woollen textiles also being important in that area. There was a certain Dutch influence in the Colchester woollen trade and it seems that Kay may have visited Holland at some stage, as his father probably did. Kay became manager of his father's mill and demonstrated his inventive genius by introducing improvements into the looms. For instance, he replaced cane reeds, through which the warp passed, by metal ones, which were much more durable and allowed the weaving of finer cloth. They became known as Kay's reeds and Kay described himself as a reed maker.

Kay's first patent, in 1730, for improving the production of yarn, was considered to be ingenious. His major invention, the flying-shuttle in 1733, was no less so. Previously, handloom weavers literally threw, with one hand, the primitive shuttle containing the weft across the loom, between the raised and lowered warps, as they had done for centuries, catching it in the other hand as it emerged, unless it was a broadloom, in which case two weavers were needed. Kay improved the shuttle design and introduced a shuttle-box at each end of the loom into which the shuttle flew. He also introduced a race, across the loom, along which the shuttle could travel, and, most important of all, a picker in each shuttle-box, both connected by cord to a picking-stick held in the weaver's right hand. By jerking the picking-stick to the left, the picker propelled the shuttle across the loom from right to left, and vice-versa. The weaver could use his left hand to pull forward the beam to push the weft into place between each crossing of the shuttle. Thus, the process was twice as fast as the traditional handloom, the shuttle crossing the loom every second, or so. With the other improvements introduced by Kay, cloth quality was improved, and only one weaver instead of two was required for the broadloom.

The weavers of Essex were not happy at what they regarded as a new gadget threatening their existence, and so, in 1738, Kay moved to Leeds. Here, he met a different problem. Users of his flying-shuttle refused to pay royalties, manufacturers combining to form The Shuttle Club to cover the costs of any member sued by Kay. So many court actions were initiated by Kay that he was almost ruined. His carding and spinning patents were lost to him and a mechanically-powered loom patented in 1745 was never exploited. Harassed by both workers and manufacturers, Kay moved back to Bury, where he fared no better. Local spinners learned of the improvements he was making to his spinning machines and a mob attacked his house in 1753. He barely escaped with his life, friends smuggling him out in a wool-sheet, but his machines and models were destroyed.

Kay's flying-shuttle seems to have been introduced into the Lancashire cotton industry around 1760, some time after its first use in the woollen industry. Kay's son, Robert, inherited or adopted at least some of his father's genius, inventing a drop-box containing three shuttles with different coloured weft, which could be used in turn in the loom, thus introducing colours into the weave. In 1764, Robert Kay wrote to the London Society of Arts, soliciting a grant for his father in recognition of his inventiveness that had greatly enriched the nation, with little recompense for the inventor. John Kay followed up his son's letter with his own, and both were referred to committees for consideration, but the following year the Society replied that the workings of the flying-shuttle were not understood by the committee.

John Kay did not pursue the issue, and no award was made. He established a new textile business in France. On the advice of the British ambassador in Paris, he seems to have returned to England in search of a just reward for his contribution to the British textile industry, but got none. He returned to France and died there in poverty and obscurity.

JAMES HARGREAVES, 1720-1778

As mentioned above, the growing popularity of the flying-shuttle caused a shortage of yarn, as the output of the spinners struggled to keep pace with the demand from the weavers. Lewis Paul, not a Lancastrian, ably assisted by his mechanic, John Wyatt, had patented a spinning machine for woollens in 1738, ending a 500-year period when spinning wheels with only one spindle were used. Although Paul made money by selling licenses for the right to use his machine, manufacturers themselves do not appear to have made handsome profits from the device. Further evidence that Paul's spinning machine was not successful in consistently producing good-quality yarn is provided by the fact that, after the patent expired, there was no rush of manufacturers to copy and use the design. In 1761, the Society of Arts offered a prize to anyone who could demonstrate an improved spinning machine producing six threads, but no satisfactory machine was forthcoming. It was left to James Hargreaves to solve the problem with his Spinning Jenny.

William E.A. Axon tells us that Hargreaves was born in 1720 in Oswaldtwistle, east of Blackburn. He was a weaver at Standhill, near Blackburn, and may have also practiced carpentry. He helped with the construction of a carding machine for Robert Peel, grandfather of the future Prime Minister, in 1760, improving a device also invented by Lewis Paul based upon the use of cylinders to comb the raw cotton into consistent strands, ready to be spun into yarn by the spinners. Blackburn, then a town of just 5,000 persons, was principally involved in producing Blackburn greys, cloth having cotton weft and linen warp, usually shipped to London to be printed. Hargreaves must have been aware of the shortage of yarn from the spinners so he set about building his Jenny, probably between 1764 and 1767. The traditional spinning machine, used for centuries, had a vertically mounted driving wheel, powered by hand, which turned one horizontal spindle. The story goes that, one day, Hargreaves witnessed a machine being knocked over, perhaps by his daughter, and continuing to work, with the driving wheel horizontal and the spindle vertical. Whatever the origin of the idea, he realised that several vertical spindles could be operated at the same time from one driving wheel. The outcome was the Spinning Jenny.

The Jenny could not spin yarn suitable for cotton warps. However, its use spread over the border into Yorkshire, where it was capable of producing both weft and warp for the woollen industry. Hargreaves first kept the Jenny secret, using it to supply his own looms with weft. The Jenny spun cotton weft on eight spindles, effectively multiplying the output of the spinner eight times, increasing to sixteen, then twenty threads in time. When news about the machine leaked out, his house was attacked and his Jennies broken by spinners who feared that they would be cast out of work. The wreckers then moved on to Robert Peel's mill. In 1767 Hargreaves and his family moved to Nottingham with his improved Jenny and he worked first with a Mr Shipley, then with Thomas James. With the latter he built a factory and, in 1770, he took out a patent on the Jenny.

Like John Kay, Hargreaves started several court actions against Lancashire manufacturers who were using his invention, and was offered £3,000 by them to compensate him, but he sought a greater settlement, asking for £7,000 and reducing this to £4,000 during negotiations. No agreement was reached and the matter headed for court, but the fact that Hargreaves had sold some Jennies to manufacturers, before patenting the invention, ruined his case. He continued as a manufacturer himself, with some success, but died on 22 April 1778. In 1779 the mob was again incensed and destroyed Hargreaves' Chorley factory. Financially, Hargreaves fared somewhat better than Kay, but fell far short of Arkwright's achievement. Hargreaves' wife received £400 for his share of the business and seems to have lived comfortably.

By 1784 there were some 20,000 hand-powered Jennies in operation, each with eighty spindles, compared with just 550 of Crompton's mules, but by then there where 143 mills in operation utilising Arkwright's water-frame. The Jenny was not amenable to being powered by water and was obsolescent by the mid-nineteenth century. James Hargreaves was long credited with the invention of the Jenny, until, in a book entitled *Compendious History of the Cotton Manufacture of 1823*, Richard Guest claimed that the Spinning Jenny had, in fact, been invented by Thomas Highs of Leigh, some time after 1767, and named after Highs daughter, Jane. Highs' Jenny had first six, then twenty, then tweny-five spindles. It should be noted that, during the case brought against Arkwright's second patent in 1785 (see below), Highs had, as an aside, claimed to have invented the Spinning Jenny. The statements of three witnesses, two written and (later) one verbal, backed the claim. It was said that Highs had developed the machine, with the help of John Kay (not the John Kay of flying-shuttle fame). In frustration at not being able to perfect it, Highs was said to have thrown his machine out of the window, but later retrieved the damaged machine and carried out further work on it. Hargreaves was said to have somehow learned of the invention and improved it, claiming it as his own. As reported below, it seems that Hargreaves may have stolen the design of Arkwright's crank and comb device, and, if this is the case, there is reason to believe that he may also have stolen Highs' design for the Jenny.

RICHARD ARKWRIGHT, 1732-1792

Richard Arkwright was born in Lord Street, Preston, on 23 December 1732, the son of Thomas, and, according to Espinasse, the youngest of thirteen children. His uncle, Richard, taught him to read, but his education was limited. He seems to have been apprenticed to a peruke (wig) maker in Kirkham, then, perhaps, a barber in Bolton. He married Patience, daughter of Robert Holt of Bolton, schoolmaster, and had one son, Richard. Patience died, and he married Margaret Biggins of Pennington, near Leigh. Arkwright established his own barber's business in Bolton and was successful in developing a wig-making business, travelling around purchasing human hair for that purpose. It seems he used to attend hiring fairs, where teenage girls, hired into domestic service, were required to have their long locks shorn!

Arkwright was not a particularly good practical engineer using his own hands, but had an excellent engineering brain. Claims that he experimented with machines in search of perpetual motion, whilst he was a barber, are probably a myth, or may have been a ruse used by him to divert attention away from his activities in the field of textile machinery, as he claimed he was developing a machine to assist in navigation. He was probably aware that Kay's invention of the flying-shuttle meant that weavers were able to work faster and use more yarn, so there was a shortage of yarn which could not be spun fast enough to satisfy the demand. Bolton depended upon Northern Ireland to provide strong linen yarns for the warps for the fustians they produced, since cotton yarn was not satisfactory. Arkwright sensed an opportunity.

As stated above, Lewis Paul had tried to produce a spinning machine in the first half of the eighteenth century, and his machine spun yarn using rollers. (Hargreaves' Jenny did not utilise rollers). Paul had the right idea, but his efforts never reached fruition. Thomas Highs of Leigh took up the challenge, aided by his neighbour and mechanic, John Kay (again, not the John Kay of flying-shuttle fame), and developed his machine between 1763 and 1766, but he did not have the drive or initiative to seek capital and exploit his machine. It appears that Arkwright heard of the invention, since he still had connections with Leigh as his father-in-law lived there.

The main feature of his machine was that it utilised sets of rollers, the roving passing through one pair of rollers, then through a second pair that was revolving faster than the first pair, thus stretching out the roving, and so on. He had returned to Preston in 1768 with the models and made contact with an old acquaintance, John Smalley, liquor merchant and painter, who agreed to help and part-fund the exploitation of the machine. It was a time of elections and riot in Preston, but the headmaster of the Free Grammar School loaned them a school house at the bottom of Stonygate, in which the machine was erected. Trials of the machine were successful, and, noting that James Hargreaves had recently been forced out of Lancashire with his Spinning Jenny by loom-breakers, Arkwright followed him to Nottingham with Smalley and Kay. He found a banker to back him and the bank directed him to Samuel Need of Nottingham and his partner, Jedediah Strutt of Derby, an important step in the exploitation of Arkwright's roller-spinning machine. Strutt had already invented, patented and benefited financially from the ribbed-stocking machine widely used in Derbyshire.

Arkwright, Need and Strutt went into partnership in 1771. Strutt had a sound business sense and a good engineering brain that enabled him to improve Arkwright's machine. Meanwhile, in 1769, Arkwright built the world's first cotton mill in Nottingham, powered by horses, and took out his

first patent for the roller-spinner. Kay left Arkwright's service in Nottingham. In 1771, a new mill was built by the River
Derwent at Cromford, in Derbyshire, powered by water.
Thus, Arkwright's spinning machine became known as the
water-frame. (In fact, the Cromford mill was driven, not by
the Derwent, but by the Cromford Sough, which drained
the Wirksworth lead mines and ran into the Derwent.) He
registered a second patent in 1775, which involved the combining of the preparation of the raw cotton prior to spinning
and the automatic feeding of such 'rovings' into the spinning
machine. Previously, the rovings had been prepared separately, and fed into the machine manually.

Initially, yarn spun on the water-frame was used in the
stocking industry, but it was now feasible to weave cloth
made entirely from British yarn, using yarn from the water-
frame for warps for the loom and yarn from Hargreaves'
Spinning Jenny for weft for the shuttle. Such cotton cloth
was termed calico cloth (the word calico is derived from
Calicut, or Calcutta, from where Indian calicoes were
exported), and, on Strutt's advice, Arkwright built a factory housing hand-loom weavers at Derby to weave it.
However, the 'Manchester Act' of 1736, which was meant
to assist the Lancashire textile industry, applied to fustians
(with cotton weft and linen warp), but not to calicoes (with
cotton weft and cotton warp), so the excise duty on calicoes
remained high in order to discourage imports from India,
and the printing of calicoes and the wearing of printed calicoes remained illegal! Thus, English calicoes were treated
in the same way as their Indian equivalents, and therefore,
initially, Arkwright and his partners had great difficulty selling the output of Arkwright's mills due to the high price. In
1774, they persuaded Parliament to rescind the 1736 Act,
and henceforth calicoes were treated as favourably as fustians, despite the opposition of Lancashire manufacturers,
who wanted to protect their own heavier cloths. Espinasse
pointed out the short-sightedness of such opposition to calicoes, describing it as 'the infant industry which, 100 years
after their opposition to it, was to clothe half the world,

enrich their descendants, and to have made their country what it is!'

After incurring £13,000 of capital expenditure, Arkwright and his partners did not begin to yield a profit until 1774, the year the Act was rescinded, but subsequent expansion of output and profit was rapid. Arkwright's second patent, granted in 1775, for the carding, drawing and roving aspects of his water-frame, were poorly specified in the patent application, for which Arkwright later had to apologise. He said, in his *Case* of 1782, that he was not trying to defraud the nation, since once the cloth started to emerge from the machines in great quantities there would be, and was, a flood of manufacturers inducing his workmen to spy on their master, pass on information on processes and even steal machinery. He said that the secrets of his inventions would not be safe, but the obscurities of his patent application were intended to stop foreign countries from stealing his inventions. It was true that, whereas he could challenge the copying of his machine in Britain, he could not do so abroad.

In 1776, Arkwright and his partners built a mill on the Derwent at Belper, Jedediah Strutt subsequently being created Lord Belper. Arkwright built Masson Mill, on the Derwent not far from Belper, and a large factory at Manchester, and licensed the machine for use in several counties, including Lancashire. Arkwright parted company with his old business associate, John Smalley of Preston, in 1777. 1779 saw a setback in the industry's fortunes, with a period of depressed trade and another outbreak of loom-breaking. At Chorley a mill was attacked, and, although the Jennies were untouched, the heavier spinning machines were wrecked. Josiah Wedgwood was in Bolton at the time, and reported seeing a large group of malcontents at Chowbent; he later learnt that a larger group of up to 8,000 people had destroyed Arkwright's mill and others at Chorley and were on their way to Cromford, with the aim of destroying mills and machinery *en route*. Fortunately, after much destruction and some deaths, the emergency subsided.

Around that time Arkwright separated from his second wife, seemingly at her instigation, ostensibly due to her unwillingness to sell a property, which they jointly owned, for £400, although following the separation she never spoke badly of him. They had one daughter. According to Baines, there was a story that his wife was annoyed with her husband spending too much time on business and too little on family, and she vented her frustrations on models of his machines, damaging them!

Arkwright's partner, Need, died in 1881 and in the same year his partnership with Strutt was dissolved, Strutt keeping the Belper mills and Arkwright keeping Cromford. Arkwright bought the estate of Willersley, near Cromford, and started to build a castle there.

Arkwright was beset by manufacturers infringing his patents and felt it necessary to take legal action against them. In 1781 he acted against nine alleged offenders, and the first of these to come to court was that against Colonel Mordaunt, whose defence was that Arkwright's specification for his 1775 second patent was obscure and not sufficiently specific, adding features that did not appear in the water-frame and not mentioning features that did. Colonel Mordaunt won his case, so the other eight of Arkwright's cases were abandoned, and thus his patent cancelled. James Watt was in Cornwall, draining tin mines with his steam engine. He wrote to a third party that he sympathised with Arkwright, whose patent was cancelled because he specified his invention wrongly. Watt said that he himself had detailed his patent specifications exactly, but he felt that he was merely teaching others how to build engines. At least Arkwright became rich whilst his patents remained valid.

In 1782, Arkwright tried to persuade Parliament to allow his second patent to run its full course, until 1789, and to extend his first patent, which was due to expire in 1783, until 1789. Parliament took no action in favour of Arkwright. In 1785, Arkwright went to court again (Arkwright versus Nightingale) to challenge an alleged infringement against his second patent, and was successful, but his victory was short-lived. Since Arkwright's second patent was cancelled in 1781, a large number of machines had been installed in many factories, and re-instatement of his patent would mean that these manufacturers would all need to pay royalties to Arkwright. A powerful combine of industrialists therefore challenged both of Arkwright's patents later in 1785.

Arkwright claimed that he had invented his machine in 1768, 'after many years' intense and painful application'. Kay, his early assistant, gave evidence at the trial. He said that in 1767 Arkwright met him at an inn in Warrington and contracted him to do some small mechanical work for him, following which Arkwright asked Kay if he could construct a model of a spinning machine, which Kay did, Arkwright paying for it and taking it to Manchester. Kay made a second model for Arkwright. He told the court that the spinning machines, using rollers, were based on Thomas Highs' invention, and that he had told Arkwright this several times. Kay was not entirely honest in his business affairs. He seems to have tried to persuade James Hargreaves that the roller-based spinning machine was his own invention, and, after working for Arkwright for several years, it appears he was accused of dishonesty in stealing tools, working on a competing machine and communicating some of Arkwright's carding secrets to James Hargreaves. As a result, Kay left Arkwright's employment and was probably resentful for that reason (and because he was never offered the partnership he sought).

Thomas Highs himself, in evidence in 1785, said that he had met Arkwright on one occasion and that he had told Arkwright that he had invented the roller spinner, but Arkwright merely said that if someone invented something, and did not exploit it, then others were free to do so. It should be noted at this point that the clockmakers and watchmakers of Lancashire, such as Kay, played an important role in developing and manufacturing the mechanical devices that revolutionised the Lancashire cotton industry.

It seemed clear that some of the accusations against Arkwright were unfounded, but the evidence of James

Hargreaves' widow, son and employee was more damaging to Arkwright's case. The crank and comb device, almost certainly invented by Arkwright, was claimed to have been invented by James Hargreaves. In fact, the opposite seems to have been true, since a business partner of Hargreaves in Nottingham later stated that he and Hargreaves had obtained the design for the crank and comb from an employee of Arkwright.

The judge's summing up was not in Arkwright's favour. Was the invention new, was it Arkwright's invention and was the specification satisfactory? The case began in the morning and lasted all day, and the jury came to an immediate decision at 1 am the next morning against Arkwright. Manchester and Lancashire rejoiced, as they were now free to use Arkwright's inventions without charge. The cotton industry surged forward with Arkwright's water-frame and Crompton's spinning mule freely available to manufacturers. The water-frame produced the cotton warp, the Jenny the coarser weft and the mule the finer weft. Prior to the water-frame and the mule, spinners had ruled the roost due to the heavy demand for their yarn from weavers, whose consumption had been speeded up by Kay's flying-shuttle. With the advent of the water-frame and the mule, the supply of spun yarn expanded rapidly and it was the weaver who became top dog. Next it was the turn of the Revd Edmund Cartwright to re-adjust the balance, with his invention of the power loom, patented in 1785.

In 1785, Arkwright, in partnership with David Dale, began building New Lanark Mills in the Clyde Valley, south-east of Glasgow. Arkwright had been recently fêted in Glasgow, with a public dinner, but after the cancellation of his second patent in 1785, he pulled out of the New Lanark project. Around the turn of the century, Robert Owen, the social experimenter, married David Dale's daughter and became involved in the historic New Lanark project. Arkwright became Sir Richard Arkwright in 1786, having presented an address to the King, congratulating him on his escape from the knife of Margaret Nicholson, and in

1787 he became High Sheriff of Derbyshire. He still played an important role in business, remained the main player in the spinning industry and was a wealthy man. He would have been even more successful had he not refused to utilise Crompton's mule for spinning finer yarn. He transferred his mill at Bakewell to his son and in 1790 he installed one of Boulton and Watt's steam engines in his mill at Nottingham and another in his Manchester factory. He also seems to have found time to improve his writing skills, which he had never mastered as a youth. Arkwright also devoted time to building his Willersley Castle and the church at Cromford, neither of which was complete when he died on 3 August 1792, aged 59, having suffered from asthma all his life. He was buried at Cromford and left an estate worth £500,000 pounds. The castle and church were completed by his son, Richard, who himself had a keen business brain and became one of the richest men in Europe.

It is generally acknowledged that Richard Arkwright did not steal inventions from others – that the water-frame was the product of his own brain. In any case, his importance lay not merely in his inventions. Crompton's spinning mule was far more important, in terms of spindles operated, than Arkwright's water-frame. Arkwright's main attributes were his drive, his ability to exploit his inventions and his competence in organising factory production. In fact, it has been said that he invented the factory system, and this was an extraordinary feat in an era when there was a great deal of opposition to factory working. He was liked by his workforce. They had to work twelve-hour shifts, although he himself led by example, working long days. He employed children, but had a policy of keeping families together. He was admired by the likes of Sir Robert Peel (father of the Prime Minister), Josiah Wedgwood and James Watt.

Perhaps one of Sir Richard Arkwright's least successful investments was his loan of £5,000 to Georgiana, Duchess of Devonshire, to help her with her gambling debts! As Amanda Harper says in Georg*iana, Duchess of Devonshire*:

The inventor Sir Richard Arkwright soon regretted his impulse to lend her several thousand pounds when she not only defaulted on her repayments but pleaded for a further loan. In January 1788 he wrote, 'I flattered myself with the hope that everything had turned out as you wished. I am sincerely sorry to find that I was mistaken.... I must also request your Grace will say whether I may rely upon the other notes being all regularly paid.... Nothing has dropt from me to any person living that could lead to suspect what your Grace wishes to remain a secret.'

SAMUEL CROMPTON, 1753-1827

Francis Espinasse tells us that Samuel Crompton, inventor of the spinning mule, was born at Firwood Farm, near Bolton, on 3 December 1753. As was common in upland Lancashire, his parents supplemented their farming incomes by carding, spinning and weaving textiles (in this locality, heavy textiles such as fustians) and selling them at the market in Bolton. His father had an inventive streak and helped build the organ gallery at All Saints, Little Bolton, even commencing construction of the organ, which was incomplete when he died, leaving his wife, Samuel, aged five, and two daughters to fend for themselves.

Before Crompton's father died, the family moved, first to a cottage nearby, then to part of Hall i'th' Wood, an ancient manor house. His mother was of sturdy stuff, and supported her family with farming, producing butter and honey, and textiles. A lame uncle lived in another room in the house; he was a hand-loom weaver. Crompton attended day-school and received a fair education, but, whilst at school and for several years as a teenager and a young man, he was obliged by his mother to participate in the textile-manufacturing activities of the household.

Hargreaves had invented his eight-spindle Spinning Jenny around 1764, and it was on such a machine that Crompton worked. The machine caused him great aggravation, and he had to spend much of his time mending broken threads. Life was a drudge, and he consoled himself by making and learning to play a fiddle. Having worked for five years with the Jenny, he became familiar with its imperfections and the poor quality of the thread that it produced. He gained insights into how these imperfections might be surmounted. Fine muslins had to be imported from India, since the warp from Arkwright's machines and the weft (for the shuttle) from Hargreaves' Jenny were too coarse to produce competing products.

At the age of twenty-two, and for five years (1774-1779) and with primitive tools, Crompton developed and experimented with a new machine, the mule, which combined and improved upon the attributes of Arkwright's waterframe and those of Hargreaves' Spinning Jenny. The mule had forty-eight spindles, compared with the Jenny's eight. Crompton seems to have been merely concerned with spinning finer yarn for himself, rather than producing machines for sale; he occasionally played the fiddle in Bolton Theatre for eighteen pence a night to supplement his income, and he worked on his machine at night, since he had to earn a living during the day, giving rise to ghost stories and gossip concerning the goings-on at the hall, which he kept secret so as to protect his invention. He was naturally solitary and unsociable, and this helped to protect his invention.

1779 was a time of riots and machine breaking, not least in the Bolton area, so Crompton made a trapdoor in the ceiling of his workroom, through which the disassembled machine could be hoisted and hidden in the attic. His mule was not discovered and he proceeded to manufacture fine yarn and, from that, fine muslins. Despite his solitariness, he met and married an accomplished spinner in 1780 and they lived in a cottage next to the hall, whilst occupying rooms in the hall for work purposes. The merchants and manufacturers of Bolton were impressed by the quality of his yarn and the demand was great, so that Crompton gave up weaving to concentrate on spinning. He continued to improve the quality of his yarn, which was equivalent to the yarns used in fine Indian Muslins, and it fetched a good price on the market.

The source of the quality yarn soon became known. The mule was not threatened by loom-breakers, since it produced quality rather than quantity, and in any case the Jenny was already popular in the Bolton area and protected from the mob. Rather, the threat to the mule came from those wishing to copy it, and Crompton was plagued by such people. Even Arkwright is rumoured to have visited, in Crompton's absence. It is a pity that the two did not meet, as Crompton was badly in need of Arkwright's business sense.

Crompton did not have the energy or the finances to patent the mule, nor did he have the drive to find a backer. He was plagued by those who wanted to discover his secret and he became desperate. Eventually he allowed himself to be persuaded by a local manufacturer, Pilkington, to put his invention into the public domain, for very little reward. Indeed, he even gave away his prototype machine. He signed an agreement with eighty local manufacturers and individuals providing that they would subscribe £67 6s 6d in total for the right to inspect and copy his mule. In the event, several signatories did not pay, despite benefiting from the invention, so that it is probable that Crompton only received some £50. He was forever disgusted with, and in contempt of, those who cheated him. In the event, he used the money to build a new mule, and this was the total benefit he received from his invention, which led to the industrialisation of Bolton and the generation of great wealth for its employers in the spinning industry.

One of the subscribing firms was Peel, Yates & Co., of Bury. Robert Peel, later knighted, son of the founder and father of the future Prime Minister, visited Hall-i'th'-Wood with some technicians and offered Crompton sixpence for each of the visitors, to pay him for his time. Crompton was incensed, and refused the offer. Crompton and his family moved to Oldhams, a farm just north of Bolton, and there Peel visited him again, twice. Peel offered him a position at the firm and even a partnership, but Crompton refused, perhaps because of the previous disagreement, or perhaps because Crompton was proud, independent and distrustful of businessmen.

At Oldhams the family continued to spin, weave and farm. Crompton tried his hand at employing spinners to increase his output, but this was not successful. He therefore concentrated on spinning the best yarn in the district and weaving it himself into the best cloth. In 1791 he moved to King Street, Bolton, using his own attic and the two attics of the adjacent houses for manufacturing purposes. He and his wife had eight children; she died in 1797.

The mule replaced Hargreaves' Spinning Jenny, and improved versions of Arkwright's water-frame only survived because they could spin heavier yarn for use on power-looms, which made their appearance in the late eighteenth century. The mule led to finer cloth being produced at a much lower price than Indian imports, which rapidly declined in quantity. With the supply of yarn increasing rapidly, there was a parallel increase in the number of hand-looms and hand-loom weavers, and, as a result, imports of raw cotton increased from 11.5 million lbs in 1784 to 56 million lbs in 1800. Much of the increase was attributable to the mule, supplemented by the Spinning Jenny and the water-frame. In this period, woollen cloth production in Lancashire was almost completely replaced by cotton textiles. By 1800, a much-improved version of the mule, the self-acting mule, had been developed by Richard Roberts, a Manchester engineer, with 400 spindles, rather than the original forty-eight. Mules with over 2,000 spindles were in use by the mid-nineteenth century

In 1800, several Manchester businessmen, led by John Kennedy, a successful Scots manufacturer who had made a fortune in Manchester – largely thanks to Crompton's mule – decided that Crompton had been poorly rewarded for his genius, and initiated a public subscription in order to better recompense him. A significant and magnanimous contributor, to the tune of thirty guineas, was Richard Arkwright, son of the inventor of the water-frame which had been largely replaced by the mule. The fund suffered from the war-time economic conditions, but raised 400 or 500 pounds, which Crompton invested in some expansion, renting the top floor of a local mill. His secrets were still sought after, by nefarious means, and, sadly, one of his sons was poached from his business by another manufacturer who wanted to discover whatever secrets Crompton still possessed.

In 1807, Crompton applied to Sir Joseph Banks and the Society of Arts for some recompense for his service to the public, but four years went by without any decision. In 1809 he learned that the Revd Edmund Cartwright had been granted £10,000 through a House of Commons Committee for his patented power-loom which had so far had only a fraction of the impact on the textile industry that the Crompton's mule had. Crompton therefore decided to do some research into the impact of his mule. He visited Scotland, where an important muslin industry had grown up, largely thanks to the mule. The grateful Scots determined to give him a public reception and dinner in Glasgow, but the shy Crompton kept his head down and left the city!

In summary, Crompton's research in 1811, presented to the Commons Committee, claimed that 4.6 million mule spindles were being operated in Britain (an under-statement), compared with 155,000 Jenny spindles and 310,000 water-frame spindles, that 70,000 spinners were working on mules and that four-fifths of the cloth woven in Lancashire utilised yarn spun on mules. In 1812, generously and ably assisted by his Manchester business community supporters, Crompton travelled to London to pursue his case, although he was too shy to appear before the Commons Committee. His case was supported by Sir Robert Peel, James Watt, Lord Stanley (Edward, later 13th Earl of Derby) and others, and the Committee decided in his favour. In the lobby of the House of Commons, Crompton was talking to Sir Robert Peel, a Lancashire Member called Blackburne and others when Prime Minister and Chancellor of the Exchequer Spencer Percival approached and commented that he thought a grant of £20,000 to Crompton should be satisfactory, asking if they agreed. Crompton left the group for a few minutes but was then conscious of an urgent rush of people – the Prime Minister had been assassinated by Bellingham! Percival had in his hand as he fell a note reading: 'Crompton, £20,000, £10,000, £5,000'.

In the event, after a delay of a few months, Lord Stanley, chairing the Committee, proposed £5,000, and this was agreed. Crompton was very disappointed, since his expenses in presenting his claim and lodging in London for four months accounted for a significant portion of the grant. His sons were critical of his management of the claim and seemed to desert him in subsequent years. Crompton established a bleaching plant at Over Darwen and went into partnership in a cotton merchant and spinning company, but neither ventures prospered, so he concentrated on his old skills.

Crompton grew poorer in old age, so in 1824, John Kennedy again initiated a public subscription and procured for Crompton an annuity of £63. Even foreign manufacturers, who had benefited from the mule, contributed to the fund. A local man, Mr J. Brown, proposed to reopen the issue in Parliament, and produced a pamphlet which detailed Crompton's claim and was signed by several businessmen. Brown went to London, but failed in his attempt to gain a further grant, and committed suicide, although the reasons are unknown.

Samuel Crompton died at home in King Street, Bolton, on 26 June 1827, aged seventy-four. He was buried in Bolton churchyard. A generation later, Bolton began to recognise the inventiveness of its son and in 1862 a statue of Crompton was erected in Nelson Square, by public subscription. The occasion was celebrated by the whole town with a gala day.

Crompton himself recognised that he did not have a business head on his shoulders. He was solitary, sullen and often depressive, especially after his treatment at the hands of those who benefited from his invention. However, his character and naive behaviour does not detract from the fact that he ought to have been better rewarded for an invention which outshone the water-frame and Spinning Jenny, which converted Bolton from a town of 5,000 people to an industrial giant of 90,000 and which was of paramount importance in the development of the Lancashire and British textile industry.

THE COTTON FAMINE, 1861-1865

Slavery had been unlawful in Britain since 1772 and, thanks to William Wilberforce and others, was abolished through-out the British Empire in 1833, with all slaves being freed in August 1834. Slavery was still legal in the Southern States of the United States of America and was a key aspect of Southern life, especially in the context of raw cotton production. The eight 'Cotton States' (Florida, Georgia, South Carolina, Alabama, Mississippi, Louisiana, Texas and Arkansas) were home to 1.8 million slaves. The South seceded from the United States largely in order to protect its right to continue to practice slavery. This secession led to Civil War, North versus South. On the eve of the American Civil War the Lancashire cotton industry was booming, as were the Southern States which were supplying the raw cotton. In 1855, the American, David Christy, wrote a book, *Cotton is King*, in which the expression 'King Cotton' was coined. In the Senate in 1858, a confident, but perhaps rather arrogant, speech argued that: 'England would topple headlong and carry the whole civilised world with her. No, you dare not make war on cotton. No power on earth dares to make war upon it – cotton is King.' According to *The Times*, 1860 was the '*annus mirabilis* of King Cotton.' The Lancashire cotton industry was, however, dependent on the United States for 85 per cent of its raw cotton imports, and, as war threatened, it was clear that the interruption of cotton supplies was a distinct possibility. The main concern, according to *The Times*, was the threat of a slave revolt, once the South seceded, but in the event the threat came not from a slave revolt but from blockade.

Soon after commencement of the American Civil War in 1861, the Federal navy blockaded the Confederate ports, from which the raw cotton harvest was exported to Britain and elsewhere. In January 1862, John O'Neill of Low Moor, Clitheroe, recorded in his diary that, some time earlier, 'The Federal Government have destroyed the harbour at Charleston by sinking ships laden with stones.' The effect was soon felt in Lancashire. Raw cotton supplies dwindled, the price of raw cotton soared and Lancashire mills started to close down. In 1860, over 2.5 million bales of cotton were imported from the Southern States, but this figure fell to only 120,000 bales in 1863. In the early nineteenth century, more Indian cotton had been imported than American, and during the Cotton Famine attempts were made to boost the Indian supply, which rose from 563,000 bales in 1860 to over 1.25 million bales in 1863. However, poor road and rail communications, poor government and cultural considerations in India prevented supply from increasing further. In any case, raw cotton from India, mainly Surat cotton, was disliked. It was termed 'the pariah of the cotton trade, the *bête noir* of the factories.' The workers hated Surat cotton. It was not as clean as American cotton, it was shorter staple, meaning that it had to be twisted more in spinning, and it was dry and brittle. In January 1862, John O'Neill of Low Moor commented that 'owing to the scarcity of cotton we are working such rubbish as I never saw in my life. We cannot do the half work that we used to.'

The Cotton Famine caused a large-scale shut-down of Lancashire cotton mills, casting hundreds of thousands of workers and their dependants into poverty and near-starvation for years. Families sold their furniture and anything else of value to raise money for their survival. Their plight was regularly and vividly reported in *The Times* by John Whittaker of Wigan, who wrote under the pseudonym 'A Lancashire Lad'. Half a million Lancastrians were affected and needed support, so a series of aid organisations were established to raise and distribute funds, including the Lancashire and Cheshire Operatives Relief Fund (in May 1862), the Central Relief Committee, the Lord Mayor of London's Mansion House Fund and 170 local relief funds. A collection was made at every church in England. By February 1863, 38.8 per cent of the population of Preston were on relief. The figures for other badly affected towns were: Ashton-under-Lyne 37.3 per cent; Manchester 29.9 per cent; Prestwich 27.8 per cent; Rochdale 26.8 per cent; Blackburn 26.5 per cent; Chorley 25 per cent; Haslingden 24.8 per cent; Bury 23.1 per cent; Oldham 21.2 per cent; Burnley 20.9 per cent; Wigan 19.6 per cent; Bolton 16.5 per cent; and Salford 15.1 per cent.

During the initial phase of the American Civil War, public opinion in Lancashire, as measured by opinions expressed at public meetings, by the press and by local Members of Parliament, was largely on the side of the Confederate States, the South, despite a commonly-held view that Lancashire selflessly supported the Federal Government, the North. Initially, Rochdale seems to have been the only textile area that supported the North, reflecting the strong views of their MP, John Bright. The reason for Lancashire's support for the South was that there was an obvious desire to see the Civil War ended and the cotton blockade raised as soon as possible, and the most likely way of achieving this seemed to be for the South to be left alone to continue exporting its cotton. The question of slavery might not have played a significant role in public opinion, as, in his inaugural speech, President Lincoln had declared that he did not intend to interfere in the institution of slavery. He was trying to pacify the South, but the effect was that neither the North nor the South seemed about to emancipate the slaves, so the moral issue of slavery stayed in the background.

Then there was the Trent incident, in December 1861, where two Confederate representatives, bound for Britain and Europe, were taken off a British ship in the West Indies by a Federal navy ship. There was outrage, and some called it an act of war. There was some sabre-rattling, as troops were sent to Canada in readiness and more were embarked at Liverpool. The situation was defused in January 1862, when the North agreed to release the two men and they arrived at Southampton in February. Britain's neutrality was firm thereafter.

The situation changed on 22 September 1862 when President Abraham Lincoln declared that all slaves, throughout the USA (including the Southern States) would be free as from 1 January 1863. Public opinion in Lancashire swung behind the North, slowly at first, but then relentlessly, as the North was perceived to have the moral advantage. The selflessness of the cotton workers who bore the suffering, whilst no longer criticising those who were responsible for imposing that suffering upon them, became legend. Lincoln described their tolerance as 'an instance of sublime Christian heroism which has not been surpassed in any age or country' and Lord Shaftesbury claimed that 'There is nothing finer on earth than a Lancashire man or a Lancashire woman.' In 1866 Gladstone told Parliament, in praise of Lancastrians, that: 'They knew that the source of their distress lay in the war yet they never uttered or entertained the wish that any effort should be made to put an end to it, as they held it to be a war for justice and for freedom'. Gladstone had already cited Lancastrians, in 1864, as exemplifying those qualities of patience and self-respect that ought to earn for them the right to vote, and under the 1867 Reform Act the franchise was duly extended to cover the male cotton workers of Lancashire, among others throughout the nation.

The ship-building industry along the Mersey flourished, providing blockade-running ships to thwart the Federal navy (and building the *Savannah* at Birkenhead for the Confederate navy). Blockade-running was a very profitable enterprise. Perhaps the most successful of the blockade-runners was Thomas Taylor, of Liverpool, who carried out twenty-eight successful expeditions. Some 1,022 blockade-running ships were captured by the Federal navy, half of all those involved, but, with cotton prices so high, two or three successful runs recouped the cost of a ship, so it seemed to be worth the risk. Blockade-runners brought out 1.25 million bales of cotton during the war, representing one-eighth of Lancashire's requirements.

At the worst point in the Famine, December 1862, the Guardians of Relief supported 485,000 people. By October

1863, this number had reduced to 167,000 and by August 1864 to 83,000. In the latter month, *The Times* was brave enough to declare that: 'The Cotton Famine is now a matter of history; it has become a thing of the past.' The final report of the Relief Committee stated that: 'There has actually been a diminution of crime under circumstances when, from compulsory idleness and poverty, an increase might have been expected.' There was less drunkenness, since workers could not afford alcohol, and this goes some way to explaining the decrease in the crime level. Strangely, despite the near-starvation of the populace, the death rate was a little lower than previously, perhaps partly due to previously-working mothers being available at home to look after their children. Marriages reduced by a quarter to a half, as presumably there was neither the money nor the inclination for couples to get married, and yet there was no increase in the level of illegitimate births. Norman Longmate, in *The Hungry Mills*, quotes from *The Times*, of 1864: 'probably no other country in the world could so peacefully and patiently have endured such a calamity.'

One amusing incident occurred in 1862, involving Henry Adams, the son of the US Federal representative in London. Adams regularly submitted articles to American newspapers, describing political and public reactions to Civil War events and issues. He strayed into social matters, and, having visited Manchester to gain first-hand experience of the situation in the North, he commented that Manchester society was more like that of American cities than London, and he compared London society unfavourably with that of Manchester. His comments found their way from the *Boston Courier* to the *Manchester Daily Examiner* and *The Times*. In London, *The Times* took up the issue, and Henry Adams was mightily embarrassed.

The Public Works Act of 1863 allowed local councils to borrow money to fund public works, and so to bring some relief to local workforces. The works campaign was ably led by an engineer, Robert Rawlinson, and, although only some 5,000 workers were employed at the most, probably fewer, it did result in the provision of sewers, drains and paved streets and roads. The work continued after the Famine was over, providing parks for recreational purposes. During the Cotton Famine, schools, sewing classes and mechanics institutes provided education and training in practical skills for idle children and adults. Sir James Kay-Shuttleworth, of Gawthorpe Hall, was prominent in the workings of relief committees (he was secretary of the Central relief Committee) and raising funds, and he channelled funds that remained unused at the end of the Cotton Famine into a Cotton Districts' Convalescent Fund, which resulted in the building of the Southport Convalescent Home and assisted cotton workers with medical expenses. Lord Derby was also prominent in fundraising and relief.

In April 1865, General Robert E. Lee surrendered at Appomattox, Virginia, and the Civil War was over. The situation in Lancashire had already been improving, slowly, and returned to normality by June 1865.

INDUSTRIAL ESPIONAGE DURING THE INDUSTRIAL REVOLUTION

Industrial espionage is not an entirely new phenomenon. For centuries, rulers and governments have sought to obtain skills, processes and machinery from other countries, often by enticing skilled workers to settle in their countries, including those persecuted for religious reasons. The export of machinery, and the encouragement of skilled artisans to take their skills overseas, was a criminal offence in England.

William E.A. Axon tells of a Belgian entrepreneur named Lievin Bauwens, who was born in Ghent in 1769, and spent his early life working in his father's leather tannery. When still a teenager he worked in a London tannery for three years, before returning to Belgium. His family were wealthy and had tanneries in various locations in Belgium. He supplied the London market and visited England several times. But his heart was not entirely devoted to the tanning industry. He was more particularly interested in engineering.

Belgium was governed by France in those days, and in 1798 Bauwens sought and received support from the French Government for his plans to learn the secrets of the Spinning Jenny (called a 'mull Jenny' in Belgium). England was ahead of Europe in cotton industry technology and Bauwens scented an opportunity. Aided by a relation, Francois de Pauw, he visited Manchester and became acquainted with a cotton-industry overseer, James Kenyon. He stayed in Manchester for some time, and married Kenyon's daughter, Mary. He procured parts of a Spinning Jenny and hid these in casks of sugar and bags of coffee, exporting these, some via Gravesend in Kent, to Hamburg.

Bauwens also recruited cotton workers to go to Belgium, taking their skills with them. However, one worker, named Harding, had a wife who objected vociferously to his departure and the plan became known to the police. Some of the prospective emigrants were arrested, but Bauwens escaped to London and then Hamburg. Sir James Crawford, the British envoy in Hamburg, attempted to have him imprisoned, but was unsuccessful. Using the machine parts already exported, and some English artisans who had emigrated prior to the plan being revealed, Bauwens was able to manufacture Spinning Jennies and set up spinning plants in Ghent and Paris, both plants being visited by Napoleon. He also operated flying shuttles. He was fêted in France and Belgium for developing the textile industry, but with the defeat of Napoleon's France, French industry was wrecked, and Bauwens ruined. He died in 1822, but is well-remembered in Ghent.

CHAPTER EIGHT

INDUSTRY, TRANSPORT
AND POPULATION

THE COAL INDUSTRY

The Romans were aware of the properties of coal. It was recovered from open-cast mine workings and has been found at several northern forts. It was used domestically – it is not difficult to imagine Roman auxiliaries from sunny Spain gaining great comfort from coal-fires on cold winter evenings in, say, Ribchester – but is more likely to have been used for industrial purposes in the North, given the availability of wood for domestic fuel. The mining of coal is recorded in the thirteenth century at Castercliffe, near Colne. In Tudor times, cannel coal was being mined in South Lancashire, as at Haigh. As already mentioned, on his travels in 1540, Leland noted that coal was being mined in Wigan, as it was in Bolton-le-Moors.

The coal was usually mined close to the surface, either in drift mines, where the entrance shaft penetrated horizontally into an exposed coal seam, usually on a hillside, or in bee-hive mines, where a shaft was sunk vertically to the level of the coal seam and the coal was then extracted, hollowing out the underground cavity until the mine became unstable. These were dangerous occupations, especially bee-hive mining. At Castercliffe, in 1514, miners were warned to fill

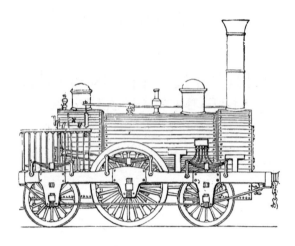

in exhausted pits to prevent humans and farm animals from falling into them. The fire-damp hazard was known, and burning sticks were dropped down the mine shaft, before the day's work commenced, to eradicate the gas, or, perhaps, a candle was burned in the mine during mining operations to consume the gas or warn of increasing gas levels.

In Tudor Lancashire, coal belonged to the landowner or leaseholder of the land, and not to the digger. It was usual to allow local residents to recover coal for their own use, or even to sell locally, but they were not allowed to sell beyond their own locality.

The development of industrial Lancashire provided an almost insatiable appetite for coal. Coal-fired steam engines were in use in ever-increasing numbers from the 1790s onwards to power the cotton industry. In the St Helens area, coal was required in large quantities in the glass-making industry. As the population of Lancashire increased, more and more coal was needed for domestic fuel and for industries such as brick-making and food processing, serving the increasing population. The Lancashire Coalfield, between St Helens, Oldham and Burnley, expanded at a rapid rate.

Mine depths increased steadily, drainage being a limiting factor. As early as 1719 a pit near Prescot was being drained with a Newcomen steam engine. Pit depths increased from 500ft in the eighteenth century to over 4,000ft by the early twentieth century. Output increased in parallel with the expansion of the Lancashire economy, reaching a peak in 1914, when 87,000 miners produced 25 million tons of coal. Decline set in after the First World War, reflecting the contraction of Lancashire industry, especially textiles, and competition from other fuel sources. Winning coal from the Lancashire Coalfield became uneconomic and uncompetitive, due to the fractured geology of the field, the lack of organisation in the industry and the availability of coal from highly-mechanised, cheap-labour coalfields overseas.

OTHER INDUSTRIES

A host of other industries flourished, largely to service the textile, coal and transport industries and the burgeoning population. The chemical industry of South Lancashire produced bleaches and dyes for the textile industry, the presence of salt in Cheshire being a decided advantage. The engineering industry produced the machines required by the textile industry, steam engines for the railways, mining equipment and a host of other products. The transport industry and the manufacture of railway engines and equipment to serve it, boomed, as did glass-manufacture, iron founding, building, quarrying, brick-making, food processing, financial services (especially in Manchester) and many more activities throughout Lancashire, supporting the world's 'first industrial society' (Chris Aspin).

Blackburn was an important loom-making centre for Lancashire and the world, and would have been even more important had Lancashire cotton manufacturers replaced their looms more frequently than they did. Some looms were still weaving 100 years after they were built. As an example, at Veevers' mill in Brierfield in the 1960s I worked on

British Northrop looms manufactured in Blackburn in
1896. Certainly they had been much improved since they
were first installed. Each loom was powered by an electric motor, instead of a steam engine through revolving
shafts, fly-wheels and belts. Each had a Unifil device fitted
that recharged the shuttle automatically with a full cop (a
bobbin of weft) when the old cop was empty, without stopping or slowing down the loom. The result of these and other
improvements was that each loom produced several times
more cloth than it did in Edwardian times, and, given the
fact that a modern weaver operated twenty-four or even
thirty-six looms, compared with the four looms operated by
an Edwardian-era weaver, the improvement in productivity
had been prodigious, but had still not been enough to compete with the rest of the world.

ROADS

Lancashire's roads in the first half of the eighteenth century
were a nightmare. They were no more than pack-horse
tracks, with deep furrows and deep mud when it rained.
Early in the century it took a week for a rider to reach
Lancashire from London, and up to two weeks for a coach
and horses, and the threat from highwaymen was ever-
present. Conditions improved when Turnpike Trusts took
over the maintenance of the major routes from local parishes
through which the roads passed. However, the turnpike era
was slow to reach Lancashire.

The first Turnpike Act for a Lancashire road was passed in
1724, some sixty years after England's first Turnpike Act, and
involved the road from Manchester to Buxton in Derbyshire.
Other turnpikes followed by the end of the century, between
Liverpool and Prescot; Wigan, Warrington and Preston;
Rochdale over Blackstone Edge into Yorkshire; Preston and
Lancaster; Salford, Warrington and Bolton; Rochdale and
Burnley; Manchester and Rochdale; Liverpool and Preston;
Clitheroe and Blackburn; Bury, Haslingden and Blackburn;

Rochdale and Edenfield; Rochdale and Bury; and others. Travelling times were cut, and it became possible to travel to London by coach in a week. Toll booths, with toll bars, were erected at points along the turnpike, and several are still recognisable, as the one at Barrowford in East Lancashire.

One quotation will serve to illustrate the problem with the roads. In his *Tour in the North of England,* published in 1770, Arthur Young said of the Preston to Wigan turnpike:

> I know not in the whole range of language, terms sufficiently expressive to describe this infernal road; to look over a map and perceive that it is a principal one, not only to some towns but even whole counties, one would naturally conclude it to be at least decent; but let me most seriously caution all travellers who may accidentally purpose to travel this terrible country, to avoid it as they would the devil, for a thousand to one but they break their necks or their limbs by overthrows or breakings down. They will here meet with ruts, which I actually measured 4ft deep, and floating with mud only from a wet summer, what therefore must it be after a winter? The only mending it in places receives, is the tumbling in some loose stones, which serve no other purpose but jolting the carriage in a most intolerable manner. These are not merely opinions, but solemn facts; for I actually passed three carts broken down in these eighteen miles of execrable memory.

The situation was significantly improved by the turnpikes, but it was not enough. Better transport facilities were badly needed.

CANALS

In the second half of the eighteenth century, Lancashire's industries were placing increasing demands on its transport system and it was clear that a new mode of transport was required. The Rivers Irwell and Mersey had been improved in 1720, providing a better link between Manchester and Liverpool. The River Douglas had been improved in the 1720s from the Wigan area northwards into the Ribble Estuary, enabling coal to be shipped to Liverpool, North Lancashire and Westmorland, and enabling Liverpool produce, and limestone and slate from North Lancashire and Westmorland, to be shipped back into the industrial areas. The Sankey Brook was improved in 1757, creating the Sankey Canal which moved coal from the St Helens area to Merseyside.

These improved river developments were not altogether satisfactory, although they demonstrated that there was a need for inland water transport and that such enterprises would profit the community generally and, hopefully, the canal owners in particular. The canal era was born.

The Duke of Bridgewater commenced building his Bridgewater Canal in 1758, from Worsley to Salford, Hollinfare and on to the River Irwell and Manchester. The aim was to deliver coal from the Duke's mines to Manchester, which objective was achieved, halving the cost of coal in the city. The canal was extended to Stretford and Runcorn on the Mersey, and was 28 miles long. James Brindley was employed in this great work, building bridges and tunnels, not least the Barton Aqueduct over the Mersey, where, for the first time in England, a vessel could sail over the top of another vessel, to the amusement of onlookers who made the aqueduct a tourist attraction of the day. Both cargo and passengers were carried on the canal.

In 1770 the construction of the Leeds-Liverpool Canal was started, stretching 128 miles from the Mersey to the River Aire, linking the Irish Sea to the North Sea, and passing through or near to Wigan, Blackburn, Accrington, Burnley and Colne, and on through the Mile Tunnel at Foulridge into Yorkshire. In 1783 the Leeds and Liverpool Canal Co. purchased the Douglas Navigation, linking Wigan to the Ribble Estuary, and from the 1790s onwards improved it with a new cut, away from the river, to create the Rufford Branch of the Leeds-Liverpool Canal from Burscough to the Ribble, together with the Leeds-Liverpool Canal proper from Burscough to Wigan. The Liverpool to Newburgh section of the canal had been completed in 1774 and the entire canal was completed in 1816 at a cost of £1 million. The canal was used to ship coal, limestone, lime, building stone, bricks and agricultural produce such as potatoes. It opened up the Lancashire Coalfield and eventually mills lined the canals wherever they passed through towns and villages. Passengers were carried, as well as freight. For instance, in 1777 regular services in packet boats conveyed passengers from Liverpool to Wigan, covering the 32 mile journey in eight or nine hours. Trippers from Wigan could alight at Scarisbrick and take a coach to Southport, and coaches met barges from Liverpool at Burscough and transported passengers on to Preston.

By 1800, canals linked Manchester to Bolton and Bury; to Ashton, Oldham and across the Pennines through the Standedge Tunnel to Huddersfield; to Rochdale and again across the Pennines into Yorkshire; to Leigh and Wigan; to Macclesfield and the Midlands; and to Runcorn and the Midlands. Preston was linked through Garstang and Lancaster Canal to Kendal. The 35-mile-long Manchester Ship Canal opened in 1894 and turned Manchester into an important inland port, with 6 miles of dock frontage. It carried ships of up to 15,000 tons into the city, through four locks raising them 60ft.

As well as providing a vital service to the industries of Lancashire, canals employed a large number of people in their construction and operation, and in associated trades such as the building of barges. They brought with them social problems; late in the nineteenth century, attempts were made to provide canal workers with houses and to get the children of canal workers to school, instead of having them work on the canals and in agriculture from an early age, as was the case previously.

RAILWAYS

Canals played a very important role in the industrial development of Lancashire, but in time they, too, were not enough. As the economy boomed, Lancashire and England were in need of a faster, more flexible mode of transport, and railways were the answer. Wooden tramways had been in existence over local distances, in several parts of the country prior to the railway age, especially in coalfields. Gravity, horses and, later, stationary steam engines provided the motive power for these tramways. The expression rail, as in railway, originates from the fact that early rails were made of wood and took their name from fence rails.

An example of the way railways developed and operated in the early nineteenth century is provided by Meyrick Bankes, a substantial landowner in the Wigan area. He built a line in order to exploit the coal found on his land. My wife's ancestral Moyers family farmed some of Bankes' land in Winstanley, and the 1838 tithe map of the area they farmed includes the names of fields and features that provide evidence of mining activity, as in Coal Pit Meadow (farmed by Agness Moyers), Coal Pit Hey, Pit Moss and Pit. In 1836, Bankes, together with his land agent, Thomas Tebay, planned and built a railway of just over 2 miles in length from Bankes' No. 2 Pit at Winstanley to the Leeds and Liverpool Canal at Wigan. (Incidentally, there was a Thomas Tebay who held a house and some fields on Bankes' Winstanley estate in 1838, and this may have been the same land agent).

On Bankes' railway, a train-load of coal of six or eight trucks transported the coal under gravity down an incline to the canal. Two horses were also carried on the train, and once the wagons were emptied, the horses pulled the wagons back up the gradient to the pit. According to Meyrick Bankes' granddaughter, Joyce Bankes of Winstanley Hall, who wrote a book entitled *A Nineteenth Century Colliery Railway*, the railway was extended, and 'the total length of rail, approximately 3.5 miles from No. 4 pit to Wigan pier head, was completed in 1845.' Her mention of 'Wigan pier head' is interesting. The point at which Bankes' railway met the canal at Wallgate Basin was known as Bankes' Pier, and it seems reasonable to conclude that this may have been, at least in part, the origin of Wigan Pier. It has to be said that Wallgate Basin on the Leeds and Liverpool Canal had been used for passenger and, probably, goods traffic for decades before Bankes' railway arrived, so Wigan Pier might have already been named at that time. Bankes' Pier was demolished in 1929. I am obliged to the Billinge History Society for much of this information. Wigan Pier was, of course, made famous by George Orwell's *The Road to Wigan Pier*. It may well be that the name was conjured up in a comic context, where, if a person was asked where he was going on his wakes week holiday, he would say that he was going to Wigan Pier if he was staying in Wigan rather than going to Blackpool or Southport.

As early as 1812 and 1816, Robert Daglish of Orrell was building steam locomotives for Orrell mine. In 1825, the Stockton and Darlington Railway in County Durham opened a new railway era, using steam locomotives as opposed to static engines and showing what was possible. The Bolton and Leigh Railway, built under the supervision of Robert Daglish and opened in 1828, utilised George Stephenson's Lancashire Witch non-static steam locomotive, but the line also used stationary steam engines and horses for those parts of the track where the incline was too great for locomotive power to surmount. The great leap forward came with the building of the Liverpool and Manchester Railway in the late 1820s, stretching 31 miles between two major centres of population. The line was entirely reliant on steam locomotives, except at the western end of the line where a static engine was required. The railway builders had to overcome several difficult obstacles. A considerable amount of material had to be sunk into the route across Chat Moss before a firm foundation was established, and at the Liverpool end of the line the Edge Hill Tunnel had to be cut.

Then the motive power had to be chosen for the line. A £500 reward was offered for a winning locomotive design.

Various locos were tested at the Rainhill Trials on 6 October 1829. The event was a milestone in the history of Lancashire and England, and 10,000 to 15,000 spectators turned up to view the bizarre spectacle. At Rainhill, near St Helens, a stretch of track was designated, measuring 1.75 miles in length. Each locomotive was expected to drive, backwards and forwards, forty times (twenty round trips), pulling a weight at least as great as three times its own weight, and achieve an average speed of at least 10 miles per hour.

The locomotives taking part in the trials were: the *Rocket*, built by George Stephenson in Newcastle-upon-Tyne; the *Novelty*, built by Braithwaite and Ericsson in London; the *Sans Pareil*, built by Timothy Hackworth in Darlingtoin; the *Perseverance*, built by Timothy Burstall in Leith; and the *Cycloped*, built by T.S. Brandreth, of Liverpool. The motive power for the Cycloped was two horses mounted on the vehicle, walking on a moving belt; not surprisingly, this could not match the performance of the steam engines. The *Perseverance* also performed poorly. The trials went on over several days. *Rocket* achieved an average speed of 24 miles per hour. Novelty achieved an average speed of 23 miles per hour, and later carried forty-five passengers at 35 miles per hour, establishing herself as favourite, but then experienced mechanical difficulties and left *Rocket* to take the £500 prize.

The Liverpool and Manchester Railway was opened with great pomp on 15 September 1830. Dignitaries present included the Prime Minister (the Duke of Wellington) and Sir Robert Peel. Unfortunately, the ceremony to mark the opening of the railway was marred by two sets of circumstances that detracted from the festive atmosphere. In the first place, among the throngs of spectators witnessing the historic sight there were demonstrations against the Corn Laws and in favour of Free Trade and an extension of the ballot. The target of the protesters was the Prime Minister, the Duke of Wellington, who was opposed to Free Trade and any extension of the suffrage.

The second circumstance was an unfortunate accident that led to the death of William Huskisson, Tory Member of Parliament for Liverpool and former President of the Board of Trade, the world's first fatal steam train accident. The Duke of Wellington and his entourage were on board the train pulled by the *Northumbrian*, driven by George Stephenson, which stopped at Parkside, Newton-le-Willows, to take on water. To impress the observers, the other locomotives performing at the opening were intended to pass the Northumbrian, 'at speed', the passengers on the stationary train being advised not to alight. However, the passengers did alight, to stroll around the track, and, as William Huskisson shook hands with the Duke of Wellington, Stephenson's *Rocket* approached, driven by Joseph Locke. Huskisson attempted to climb back into his carriage, but stumbled in his haste and was hit by the *Rocket*, which severed his left leg. The *Northumbrian*, minus most of its carriages and dignitaries, took Huskisson to Eccles, where the unfortunate politician expired in the vicarage that evening.

The Liverpool and Manchester Railway showed what could be achieved. Prior to the opening of the railway, 14,000 travellers per annum had been carried by coach between Liverpool and Manchester. The coming of the railway raised the numbers travelling between the cities to 500,000, to which could be added the large quantity of freight. In *Observations on a General Iron Railway*, Thomas Grey proposed that the Liverpool and Manchester should be used as a prototype for a national railway network, but, with or without Grey's influence, a railway boom ensued. James Gilbert's *A New Railway Map of England and Wales*, dated 1839, shows that in those nine elapsed years, Railway Acts had passed through Parliament for the main north-south route from Scotland between Warrington, Wigan, Preston and Lancaster, for the Preston to Fleetwood line, the Manchester to Bolton line and the Manchester to Halifax and Leeds line, as well as the earlier Liverpool to Manchester line. The route to Scotland beyond Lancaster, over Shap Fells, was in the planning stage. There had been doubts that steam power could scale Shap, and Sir Peter Hesketh Fleetwood had planned to sail railway travellers to Scotland from Fleetwood, where the railway arrived in 1840. However, Shap was conquered and Fleetwood was relegated in status to that of a secondary route.

The canal era had demonstrated that physical and geographical obstacles could be overcome, with imagination and ingenuity. Canal engineers and their pupils were now ready to turn their attention towards railway building, confident in their own ability. The canal era also left a breed of navvies to build the railways. 1845 marked the start of Railway Mania, a period during which there was a large and rapid expansion of railway building. By the end of this period Lancashire's railway network was virtually complete. The main West Coast line to Scotland ran right through the county, north to south, Manchester and Liverpool were the centres of radiating rail networks, lines served the coastal towns and resorts, Morecambe Bay was rounded, all the main industrial towns were linked and several lines crossed the Pennines into Yorkshire. Great railway company names abounded, as smaller companies merged or were taken over during a period of consolidation – the Lancashire and Yorkshire Railway, the East Lancashire Railway (which became part of the L&YR), the London and North Western Railway, the Furness Railway. Even the Midland Railway penetrated from Skipton to Colne and the Great Central from Sheffield to Manchester.

A Lancashire man, Sir Edward William Watkin, played a prominent role in the attempt to drive the first railway tunnel under the English Channel, an enterprise that foundered in 1882 due to opposition from vested interests, and security fears. Edward Watkin was born in Manchester in 1819, son of the diarist and cotton trader Absalom Watkin. Edward became an accomplished railway proprietor and promoter in Britain, Canada, Greece and India. He became Member of Parliament for Stockport and was an agitator for the abolition of the Corn Laws and the introduction of half-day working on Saturdays. He proposed a railway tunnel from Scotland to Ireland and he planned a pleasure park on the current site of Wembley Stadium in London, complete with a tower reminiscent of the Eiffel Tower. Neither project bore fruit.

Edward Watkin became chairman of the Channel Tunnel Co., and the embryonic tunnel extended almost 2 miles under the Channel from Shakespeare Cliff in Kent. On a less ambitious scale, Watkin established a footpath to the summit of Mount Snowdon, from his holiday cottage to the south-east of the mountain. The footpath bears his name, and was opened by Prime Minister William Gladstone in 1892. Watkin was also involved in Charles Dickens' visits to Manchester on charitable business.

Another attempt to link the railways of England with those of the continent emerged during the Edwardian era, but this time further north and by ship. The enterprising Lancashire and Yorkshire Railway attracted tourists from the Continent by ferrying them from Zeebrugge, Antwerp and Rotterdam to Hull and Goole in L&YR ships such as the *Duke of Clarence*, the *Mellifont* and the *Hebble*. Passengers were then transported by rail to tourist attractions in Lancashire and Yorkshire, and perhaps even from Fleetwood to Belfast on board the *Duke of Connaught*. A series of L&YR postcards, the 1907 Series, was issued featuring the ships themselves and tourist destinations, such as Blackpool, St Annes, Southport, Towneley Hall in Burnley, Whalley Abbey, Gawthorpe Hall near Burnley, and so on. The postcards designated the railway stations serving these attractions. For foreign visitors, the postcards were overprinted with a French legend, extolling the virtues of the places featured, these cards being sent to family and friends by the visitors either from England or on their return to the Continent.

Appropriately, the last scheduled passenger steam train journey in England ended at Liverpool Exchange Station on 3 August 1968, having been pulled by a Black Five engine from Preston.

POPULATION

Trade accelerated in the nineteenth century, after being restricted during the wars of the eighteenth and early nineteenth centuries. As a reflection of booming industry and trade, the population of Lancashire rose rapidly, from perhaps 100,000 in the mid-sixteenth century, to 673,000 in 1801, to 1,336,000 in 1831, to 2,026,000 in 1851, to over 3 million in 1881 and to 4,800,000 in 1911. By 1951 the population of the county had reached 5,100,000, 9 per cent of the population of the United Kingdom, the large majority living south of the River Ribble. As an example of the influx of population, at the 1851 Census 25 per cent of the population of Lancashire was reportedly born outside the county. Some of my own ancestors came to live in the county during the nineteenth century from Ireland, Cumberland and Yorkshire. Lancashire was where the work was.

The population became largely urban as towns expanded astonishingly. In 1801 there were ten towns with a population of over 10,000. By 1851 that number had grown to seventeen and by 1901 to seventy-three. Manchester/Salford increased in population from 112,000 in 1801 to 529,000 in 1861. Preston, the first town outside London to have its streets lit by gas lights (in 1815), had a population of 12,000 in 1800, growing to 90,000 by 1868, mostly directly or indirectly reliant on the town's twenty-seven mills for their livelihood. Bolton expanded from 11,000 in 1791 to 105,000 in 1881. Wigan's population grew from 25,000 in 1801 to 78,000 in 1861, many of them being involved in mining the 6 million tons of coal that the area produced, annually. Barrow-in-Furness had a population of only 300 in 1847, when the railway arrived, but this increased to 70,000 in the late nineteenth century, thriving on the local mining of iron ore and the development of its iron-works.

The population of Liverpool expanded from 77,000 in 1801 to 269,000 in 1861, thriving on the triangular West African and West Indies trade, including the slave trade, and the import of raw cotton from the United States. The slave trade commenced around 1730. Manufactures were exported to the Guinea Coast of Africa, slaves were then shipped from the Guinea Coast to the West Indies, and sugar, rum and tobacco were shipped from the West Indies to Liverpool. The slave trade helped to make Liverpool a rich city, with one-quarter of its ships being involved in slaving in 1790. However, William Roscoe, MP for Liverpool, voted for the abolition of the slave trade in Britain in 1807 and was successful in his quest.

Britain's first artificial, enclosed dock was built in Liverpool in 1715. Liverpool surpassed Bristol in importance as a port in the mid-eighteenth century, had 2 miles of docks by 1835 and 6 miles by late nineteenth century. In 1814, the first ship sailed from Liverpool to India around Cape of Good Hope, carrying cheap calico cloth, after the East India Co. lost its monopoly of Indian trade. The ship's captain was Sir John Gladstone, father of the future Liberal Prime Minister, William Gladstone (born in Liverpool). The import of US cotton commenced in the late eighteenth century. In 1834, 839,000 bales of raw cotton were imported, and by 1868 imports had increased to 3,326,000 bales. Liverpool handled 4,781 vessels carrying 510,000 tons of cargo in 1802, 12,928 vessels carrying 1,540,000 tons of cargo in 1832, and 20,289 vessels carrying 4,630,000 tons of cargo in 1862.

CHAPTER NINE

MODERN TIMES, MID-NINETEENTH CENTURY TO 1945

LATE VICTORIAN AND EDWARDIAN ERA

The second half of the nineteenth century and the Edwardian period saw Lancashire reach its zenith in terms of economic activity. As has been noted, the population of the county more than doubled between 1851 and 1911, almost reaching its modern level of around 5 million. Lancashire's astonishing rate of growth enabled this increased population, including large numbers of emigrants from Ireland, to be absorbed. Cotton textiles output peaked in 1912 and coal output peaked in 1914. As well as the old industries, there were examples of significant new developments, as at Barrow-in-Furness, where the maritime location and railway communications, together with local iron ore and associated iron and steel industry, led to the establishment of shipbuilding from 1850 onwards. In 1897, Vickers took over ownership of the shipyards and during the 1890s and Edwardian period the yards were busy building warships for customers around the world, including Dreadnought battleships for the Royal Navy and the Navy's first submarine. In a sense, Lancashire had reached a plateau of economic achievement, especially compared with the rest of the country, and thereafter had to work hard to maintain its position in the world as its old industries declined.

Queen Victoria died in 1901 and was succeeded by her son, King Edward VII (1901-1910), initiating the Edwardian era that is generally accepted as lasting up to the commencement of the First World War, 1914. It is tempting to think of the Edwardian era as a golden epoch in Lancashire's history, with high employment and high output. It is true that poverty remained a prevailing condition in many areas, but the image of holidaymakers visiting Blackpool or Southport and sending home postcards in their millions is an enduring one. I can imagine my grandmother, skipping happily in the school yard or backstreet in the latter days of the Boer War (1899-1902), chanting the following contemporary skipping rhyme that she recounted to me:

Lord Roberts and Kitchener, Baden Powell and White
All went off to Africa to have a jolly good fight;
When the war is over how happy we will be,
We'll raise the flag at Pretoria and Kruger hang on a tree.

We did raise the flag at Pretoria, but by that time President Kruger had left South Africa and did not meet the fate wished upon him by unknowing schoolgirls and others.

THE SINKING OF THE *TITANIC*

King Edward VII died in 1910 and his son inherited the throne as King George V (1910-1936). This was to be a tumultuous period in the history of Europe, but one tragic episode in 1912, before the onset of war, affected Lancashire and Britain deeply. The White Star Lines passenger liner, *Titanic*, sailed from Southampton, hit an iceberg and sank in the North Atlantic. In the modern version of the film *Titanic*, as the ship was sinking, with the band playing, one of the bandsmen addressed the bandmaster as 'Wallace'. The attention to detail was impressive. The bandmaster on the Titanic was indeed 'Wallace': Wallace Henry Hartley.

Wallace Hartley was born in Colne in 1878 and showed early musical promise. He played in several bands and joined Cunard as ship's bandmaster. He made eighty crossings of the Atlantic on the *Mauretania* and *Lusitania*, and was invited to conduct the small orchestra on the maiden voyage of the *Titanic*, a tribute to his ability of which he was no doubt proud.

The *Titanic* sank on 14/15 April 1912, with the loss of 1,517 lives, and as she went down Wallace and his seven bandsmen played on. Tradition has it that they played 'Nearer My God To Thee'. Wallace's body was recovered from the sea and he was buried in Colne, where his memorial displays a violin carved on its base. A thousand mourners attended his funeral, seven bands led the procession to the cemetery and an estimated 40,000 people lined the streets to pay their respects. A monument to the memory of Wallace Hartley stands on Albert Road, Colne, a fitting tribute to a local hero. There is a plaque to the memory of the eight lost musicians in the Philharmonic Hall, Liverpool, one of them being bass violinist Fred Clarke, a native of Liverpool. There is also a monument on the Liverpool waterfront to 244 engineers who lost their lives on the ship.

More can be said about the *Titanic* and its Lancashire connections (with acknowledgements to Jonas Holdsworth and *The Lancashire Magazine*, March 2009). She was built by

Harland and Wolff in Belfast, was registered in Liverpool and sailed from Southampton on her maiden voyage. She was owned by White Star Line, whose headquarters was the White Star Building in Liverpool. Second Officer Charles Lightoller, from Chorley, was in charge of loading lifeboats on the port side and distinguished himself by applying the 'women and children first' policy. He was with the ship when it went down, apparently trying to assemble a canvas-sided collapsible lifeboat, and was sucked under, but was then propelled to the surface by a pocket of air escaping from the ship. He was able to climb onto an upturned lifeboat, helping thirty others to scramble aboard, and survived to be rescued, being perhaps the last of the survivors to board the *Carpathia*. His contribution to maritime safety did not stop there. He later recommended that, in future, all ships should carry enough lifeboats to accommodate all passengers and crew.

Lightoller served in the Royal Navy in the First World War and commanded a destroyer that rammed and sank a U-boat. He was awarded two Distinguished Service Crosses for bravery. Almost thirty years later, he further distinguished himself by captaining one of the 'little ships' at the miracle of Dunkirk, using his own boat, *Sundowner*, to rescue 139 soldiers and bring them back to England.

Another Lancastrian aboard the *Titanic* was Fred Fleet, the lookout who first saw the iceberg. One man who did not emerge from the tragedy with the reputation of a hero was Joseph Bruce Ismay, from Crosby, Chairman and Managing Director of White Star Line. It seems to have been his decision to reduce the number of lifeboats on the ship from the planned forty-eight to the minimum required by regulations, sixteen, in order to save space and perhaps reduce weight. Ismay sailed on the ship and survived. It appears that he helped women and children onto a lifeboat, and, there being no other passengers at that point needing a place, he and several other men then boarded the same lifeboat. He was castigated by public opinion for abandoning ship and leaving 1,500 others, including women and children, to die.

The rescue ship *Carpathia* was 60 miles away when it picked up the distress message from the *Titanic*. The wireless operator of the *Carpathia* immediately alerted his captain, Arthur Henry Roston, a Lancastrian, born in Astley Bridge. Captain Roston sailed to the rescue without delay, picking up 712 survivors. He was fêted in Britain and in the USA for his efforts, and was ultimately knighted.

At the other end of the spectrum, a native of Bolton, Captain Stanley Lord of the SS *Californian*, had his reputation ruined that night. As his ship approached ice, he ordered his wireless operator to warn other ships of the danger, and stopped the ship until dawn, a wise precaution. The captain and sole radio officer retired for the night. During the night, officers and seamen on the *Californian* were reported to have seen white rockets being fired from a distant ship. Apparently, they woke Captain Lord several times in the night, reporting what they had seen, but he took no action. Perhaps he thought it was a party on board the *Titanic*. Presently, with no lights visible from the sinking ship, the *Californian* steamed away, only returning to join the *Carpathia* in the search for survivors when notified of the tragedy by another ship. Captain Lord later claimed that he was 17 to 20 miles away from the *Titanic* and saw no rockets, but, if he had immediately gone to the rescue, more lives might have been saved. He was not formally blamed for the incident, but this did not stop him from being vilified and possibly used as a scapegoat. Captain Stanley Lord died in 1962, but in 1996, as a result of a libel action in connection with a book, his name was finally cleared.

THE FIRST WORLD WAR AND THE DEPRESSION

The horrors heaped on Lancashire's manhood by the First World War are exemplified by the plight of the Accrington Pals, a battalion of volunteers from Accrington, Blackburn, Burnley and Chorley. On the first day of the Battle of the

Somme, on 1 July 1916, 235 of the Pals were killed and 350 wounded, out of a total strength of 700. Edward Stanley, 17th Earl of Derby, played a role in establishing the 'pals' principle of recruitment, and carried out a successful recruitment campaign in Liverpool at the beginning of the war. In 1915, whilst favouring conscription, he investigated whether or not volunteers could satisfy the army's demands for manpower through a system of attestation. Lord Derby had already been Conservative Member of Parliament for Westhoughton and served in the governments of Lord Salisbury and Arthur Balfour in the 1890s and early 1900s. He was known as the un-crowned King of Lancashire, because of his influence. He became Secretary of State for War from 1916 to 1918, though he was neither strong nor effective in this role, except, perhaps, in the field of recruitment.

The First World War was a watershed in Lancashire's fortunes. A brief post-war boom was enlivened by the first crossing of the Atlantic by air from Newfoundland to Ireland by John Alcock and Arthur Whitten Brown in 1919. Alcock was from Manchester and Brown was living in Manchester but was born in Glasgow, of American parentage. They flew in a modified Vickers Vimy First World War bomber and were fêted in Manchester.

The brief post-war boom was followed by recession during much of the 1920s, leading into the Great Depression of the 1930s. The twentieth century decline of the cotton textile industry has already been outlined. The industry suffered from loss of foreign markets and poor industrial organisation and investment. Textile exports fell by three-quarters between 1912 and 1938 and textile employment fell by over 35 per cent. The mining industry followed cotton into decline as a result of lower demand from cotton mills, geological constraints in the coalfields and again lack of industrial organisation. The miners' strike of 1926 triggered the General Strike, which lasted for ten days in May, 1926, but the miners stayed out for six months. For much of Industrial Lancashire there was no ready alternative employment, and unemployment rates soared, in some places to

30 per cent or more. One bright spot was the development of Trafford Park Industrial Estate, alongside the Manchester Ship Canal, with its welcome injection of diversification into the Lancashire economy, especially in the field of electrical engineering.

For the working man (and some working women), sport was a pleasurable distraction from the harsh realities of industrial life. Lancashire teams featured prominently in the Football League, founded in 1888, six of the twelve founding member-teams being Lancastrian – Accrington Stanley, Blackburn Rovers, Bolton Wanderers, Burnley, Everton and Preston North End. They were joined by Manchester United, Manchester City, Liverpool, Wigan, Blackpool, Barrow, Southport, Rochdale, Oldham and Nelson. Rugby League was popular in South Lancashire.

Cricket was also popular. A Lancashire county team was formed in 1864 and played at various grounds around the county. The first 'Roses' match between Lancashire and Yorkshire was played at Station Road, Whalley, in 1867 – Yorkshire won. The Lancashire League, the Central Lancashire League and the North Lancashire and Cumbria League were founded in 1892. The Lancashire League included teams based in and around East Lancashire – Accrington: Bacup, Burnley, Church, Colne, East Lancashire (Blackburn), Enfield, Haslingden, Lowerhouse, Nelson, Ramsbottom, Rawtenstall, Rishton and Todmorden. Each team included a professional player, the most successful of whom was Learie Constantine, 'Connie', who played for Nelson from 1929 to 1937 and who was probably the best paid of all sportsmen in all sports in England at the time, earning as much as £750 per annum. He was a legend, born in Trinidad, the grandson of slaves. He played international cricket for the West Indies. He was unimpressed by the Lancashire weather, especially the drizzle! The Constantines lodged for a time with some distant relatives of mine in Nelson and my grandmother and grandfather used to visit them.

Constantine was a huge crowd-puller. 'Gates' of 8,000 to 10,000 were common at Seedhill, Nelson, and he once attracted a crowd of 14,000 to Bacup. Presumably, Constantine was the darling of cricket club treasurers within the League. It has been calculated that during the 1929 to 1933 period, Nelson was involved in 15 per cent of the games played, home and away, within the League, but this 15 per cent of games accounted for 75 per cent of the gate receipts for the League members during that period. The crowds certainly turned out to see Connie. There is a tale that, on the dismissal of Connie for a low score, a spectator complained to the bowler that 'we've come to see him bat, not thee ball'. He became a governor of the BBC and was a member of the Race Relations Commission. He was awarded an MBE, was made freeman of Nelson, was knighted and became Lord Constantine ('Baron Constantine of Maraval in Trinidad and Tobago, and Nelson in the County Palatine of Lancashire'). He was invited by Jeremy Thorpe to stand as the Liberal Party Parliamentary candidate for Nelson and Colne but declined the offer.

THE SECOND WORLD WAR

King George V died in 1936, and, following the abdication of his son, Edward VIII in the same year, George VI became King and reigned over a country fast approaching war. As with the First World War, 1939-1945 was an economic watershed for Lancashire, finally bringing to an end the Great Depression and ushering in an era of fuller employment and strategically dispersed modern war industries that are still important to the economy of the county. Examples of companies introduced or greatly enhanced by wartime activities are British Aerospace (now BAE SYSEMS) at Warton, west of Preston, Samlesbury and Chadderton; Rolls-Royce at Barnoldswick (then in Yorkshire but providing employment for Lancastrians); Lucas at Burnley and Vickers in Barrow-in-Furness. A host of suppliers served these companies, many such suppliers starting life in Lancashire's redundant cotton mills. The Swan and Royal Hotel in Clitheroe was the venue

of a meeting between company executives in 1942 that saw
Rolls-Royce take over the jet engine business of Rover at
Barnoldswick, a historic development.

Lancashire did not escape the attentions of the Luftwaffe
during the war. Liverpool was bombed often, notably just
before Christmas 1940 and again in May 1941. Some 4,000
people lost their lives. Manchester and Salford were also
bombed just before Christmas 1940, leaving 560 dead.
Barrow-in-Furness was hit in April-May 1941, with the loss
of eighty-three lives.

One of the most tragic incidents of the war in Lancashire
happened in 1944 at Freckleton, on the Ribble Estuary, just
west of Preston. For much of the Second World War, the
people of Freckleton might have considered themselves to
be fairly far-removed from the horrors of the Front Line and
from the nightmare of the Blitzkriegs inflicted on our cities.
Of course, they were subject to wartime austerity, some of
their sons and daughters were serving in the forces and there
was an American air-base on their doorstep, just to the west,
at Warton. But, as I paid my respects at the site of the tragedy, I could only imagine that they must never have dreamt
that the war could so suddenly impose itself on them in such
a horrific manner. In retrospect, the fact that the disaster was
an accident, only indirectly the result of war, renders the loss
even more tragic.

On the morning of 23 August 1944, a B-24 Liberator
bomber of the US Air Force was on a test flight, having been
refurbished at Base Air Depot 2 at Warton. The plane was
in company with another Liberator. With seemingly little
warning, a violent storm approached Warton and the two
planes were ordered back to base. As the aircraft approached
the airfield from the west, the weather deteriorated to such
an extent that they decided to abort the landing and fly north
to wait for the storm to pass. However, due to the violence
of the stormy weather (or perhaps due to what we now call
wind-shear), the first Liberator lost control and crashed in
Freckleton at around 10.47 a.m., demolishing the 'Sad Sack
Snack Bar' and running on into the infant section of Holy

Trinity School, where the plane, and the spilled fuel around it, erupted in flames. Thirty-eight pupils and two teachers died as a result of the accident, plus the three crewmembers of the Liberator and eighteen people in the snack bar (four RAF personnel, seven US Air Force personnel and seven civilians), sixty-one deaths in all.

The two teachers and most of the children were buried in Holy Trinity churchyard, where there is a fitting memorial. Nearby is a memorial garden and playground, created with funds raised by the US Air Force Base Air Depot 2 at Warton. A stone memorial tablet in the garden reads:

> This playground presented to the children of Freckleton by their neighbors of base air depot No. 2 USAAF in recognition and remembrance of their common loss in the disaster of August 23rd 1944.

I found the memorials greatly moving. I have myself visited Warton airfield, now operated by BAE SYSTEMS, on several occasions, and flown into and out of it once, but was not aware at the time of the Freckleton disaster. Had I been aware, I would have certainly visited the memorials many years ago. I am pleased to acknowledge that I have gleaned source material for the above from the website of the Lancashire Aircraft Investigation Team, and specifically from an article entitled 'The Freckleton Disaster' on that website.

I mentioned the film *Titanic* previously. There are two other classic films that I know of with Lancashire connections. The first is *Whistle Down the Wind*, filmed in and around Downham, in the lee of Pendle, in 1961. The second film is *Brief Encounter*, filmed partly on Carnforth station in 1945. Carnforth, in North Lancashire, is on the main West Coast Line from London to Glasgow. Charles Nevin, in his *Lancashire, Where Women Die of Love*, quotes star Celia Johnston as saying that, in between shooting, she spent much time in the station buffet, 'rushing out now and again to see the expresses roaring through'. I remember train-spotting on Carnforth station around 1960 myself. When an express was due to pass through, without stopping, a warning bell would ring, continuously and ominously. We would be ushered back from the platform edge to a point maybe 10ft away. The *Royal Scot*, the *Midday Scot* or the *Caledonian* expresses would hurtle through at 70 miles an hour, maybe more, with an enormous amount of noise, draught, steam and smoke. So, I'm not alone in finding the age of steam exciting.

Brief Encounter was written by Noel Coward and also starred Trevor Howard. To be honest, only about 10 per cent of *Brief Encounter* was filmed on Carnforth station. It would have been more, had the sequences inside the café been filmed there, but these were shot back at the studio. The age of steam has gone, and electric trains continue to hurry through *en route* to and from Scotland, but the station fell into disrepair, until an enthusiast called Peter Yates, together with the Carnforth Station and Railway Trust, carried out renovation work. Even the original clock was located and returned to the station, which is now a tourist attraction.

AND FINALLY

It seems somehow appropriate that *The Brief History of Lancashire* should end with a 'Brief Encounter' at Carnforth Station! On the one hand, Carnforth is the end of the line for us, the parting of the ways, just as it was for Celia Johnston and Trevor Howard. On the other hand, Carnforth station's under-recognised role in the history of cinema reflects the under-recognised role of Lancashire and Lancastrians in certain aspects of national and world history. I am thinking here, for instance, of the part played on the national stage by the Stanley/Derby family, whose role in English history, according to the topographical writer and historian Jessica Lofthouse, has long been under-played in national histories. I hope that this history does something to set this imbalance to rights.

BIBLIOGRAPHY

I list below most of the sources that I have drawn from in writing this book. I am indebted to the authors of these works and to the other organisations listed. Inevitably, I have referred to more sources than are listed here, and have not found it feasible to list every one. I apologise to any authors whose works I have used but inadvertently not acknowledged.

Ackroyd, Peter, *Dickens*, Sinclair-Stevenson, 1990.

Addison, William, *In the Steps of Charles Dickens*, Rich & Cowan, 1955.

Ainsworth, W. Harrison, *The Lancashire Witches*, George Routledge & Sons, *c.* 1875.

Aspin, Chris, *The Cotton Industry*, Shire Publications, 1981.

Aspin, Chris, *The First Industrial Society*, Helmshore Local History Society, 1969.

Axon, William E.A., *Echoes of Old Lancashire*, William Andrews, 1899.

Axon, William E.A., *Lancashire Gleanings*, Tubbs, Brook & Chrystal/ Simpkin, Marshal & Co., 1883.

Bagley, J.J., *A History of Lancashire*, Phillimore, 1976.

Bennett, Walter, *The History of Marsden and Nelson*, Nelson Corporation, 1957.

Bloy, Dr Marjorie, A Web of English History, http://www.historyhome. co.uk/

Brigg, Mary (ed), 'The *Journals of a Lancashire Weaver*', The Record Society of Lancashire and Cheshire, Vol. CXXII, 1982.

Britten, Nick, *The Daily Telegraph*, 9/4/2009

Bryson, Graeme, *Shakespeare in Lancashire*, Sunwards Publishing, 1997.

Carver, Stephen, *The Life and Works of Lancashire Novelist William Harrison Ainsworth, 1805-1882*, Edwin Mellen Press LTD, 2003

Collingwood, R.G., *Roman Britain*, Oxford University Press, 1970.

Collins, Herbert C., *Lancashire Plain and Seaboard*, J.M. Dent & Sons, 1953.

Coombs, David G., 'Excavations at the Hill Fort of Castercliff, Nelson, Lancashire, 1970-71', *Transactions of the Lancashire and Cheshire Antiquarian Society*, 1982.

Cromarty, Deas, *Picturesque Lancashire (North of the Ribble)*, 1906.

Dexter, Walter, *The England of Dickens*, Cecil Palmer, 1925.

Dickens, Charles, *George Silverman's Explanation*, Chapman & Hall, 1868.

Dickens, Charles, *Hard Times*, Chapman & Hall, 1854.

Dobson, Bob (ed), *Really Lancashire magazine*, May 1996.

Dolby, George, *Charles Dickens As I Knew Him*, T. Fisher Unwin, 1885.

Edwards, B.J.N., *Ribchester*, Ribchester Museum Trust, Lancashire.

Espinasse, Francis, *Lancashire Worthies*, Simpkin, Marshall & Co., 1874.

Espinasse, Francis, *Lancashire Worthies*, Second Series, Simpkin, Marshall & Co., 1877.

Falkowski, Paul, Rutgers University, New Jersey, USA, *Sunday Times*, 9/11/2008.

Feiling, Keith, *History of England*, Book Club Associates, 1950.

Fishwick, Lt. Col. Henry, *A History of Lancashire*, Elliott Stock, 1894.

Fordham, Amanda, *Georgiana, Duchess of Devonshire*, Harper Collins Publishers, 1998.

Forster, John, *The Life of Charles Dickens*, Chapman & Hall, 1911.

Foxe, John, *Book of Martyrs*, *c.* 1583, various editions

Gaskell, Elizabeth, *The Life of Charlotte Brontë*, 1857, republished, intro. by Winifred Gerin, The Folio Society, 1971.

Goffin, Magdalen (ed), *The Diaries of Absalom Watkin*, Alan Sutton, 1993.

Gooderson, P.J., *A History of Lancashire*, B.T. Batsford, 1980.

Griffith, T. Meirion, 'No. 84 Plymouth Grove, the Manchester Home of Mrs Gaskell', *Transactions of the Lancashire and Cheshire Antiquarian Society*, 1982.

Hewlett, E.G.W., *A History of Lancashire*, Oxford University Press, 1934.

Hill, Lawrence, *Gentlemen of Courage – Forward...*, Magnolia Publishing Company, 1987.

Holden, Anthony, *William Shakespeare – His Life and Work*, Abacus, 2000.

Holdsworth, Jonas, *Titanic – The Lancashire Connection*, The Lancashire Magazine, March 2009.

Holt, Geoffrey, O. *A Regional History of the Railways of Great Britain*, Vol. 10, The North West, David & Charles, 1978.

Howat, Gerald, *Learie Constantine*, George Allen & Unwin/Readers Union Ltd., 1976.

Ince, Henry (ed), *The Wonders of the World in Nature and Art*, Grattan & Gilbert, *c.* 1840.

Kaplan, Fred, *Dickens – A Biography*, Hodder & Stoughton, 1988.

King, Jonathan, *The Mayflower Miracle*, David & Charles, 1987.

Kitton, Frederick G., *Charles Dickens*, The Caxton Publishing Company.

Kitton, Frederick G., *The Dickens Country*, Adam & Charles Black, 1911.

Lancashire Aircraft Investigation Team – The Freckleton Disaster.

Langshaw, Arthur, *A Guide to Clitheroe Castle*, The Kaydee Bookshop, Clitheroe, 1947.

Ley, J.W.T., *The Dickens Circle*, Chapman & Hall, 1918.

Lofthouse, Jessica, *Lancashire's Fair Face*, Robert Hale, 1976.

Lofthouse, Jessica, *Lancashire Landscape*, Robert Hale, 1951.

Lofthouse, Jessica, *Lancashire's Old Families*, Robert Hale, 1972.

Lofthouse, Jessica, *Three Rivers*, Robert Hale, 1949.

Longmate, Norman, *The Hungry Mills*, Maurice Temple Smith, 1978.

Marshall, J.D., *Lancashire*, David & Charles, 1974.

Mee, Arthur, *The King's England – Lancashire*, Hodder & Stoughton, 1949.

Mills, David, *The Place Names of Lancashire*, B.T. Batsford, 1976.

Mitchell, Alan, *A Short History of Winstanley Hall and Estate*, the Billinge History Society, 2002.

Moorwood, Helen, 'Helen's Story, from Duxbury to Shakespeare', http://www.duxbury.plus.com/bard, 2004.

Moorwood, Helen, 'Pilgrim Father Captain Myles Standish of Duxbury, Lancashire and Massachusetts,' http://www.mylesstandish.info

Nevin, Charles, *Lancashire, Where Women Die of Love*, Mainstream Publishing, 2006.

Osborne, E. Allen, *The Facts About A Christmas Carol*, The Bradley Press, 1931.

Owen, Sharran, 'Granny Tales', *Magazine of the Lancashire Family History & Heraldry Society*, August 2006.

Peel, Edgar & Southern, Pat, *The Trials of the Lancashire Witches*, David & Charles, 1972.

Philip's Concise Atlas of the World, 2007.

The Pilgrim Edition – *The Letters of Charles Dickens, Vol. 1*, House, Madeline and Storey, Graham (eds), Oxford University Press.

The Pilgrim Edition – *The Letters of Charles Dickens, Vol. 7*, Storey, Graham, Tillotson, Kathleen and Easson, Angus (eds), Oxford University Press, 1993.

Pilkington, Martin, 'The Brontës' Lancashire Bounty', *Lancashire Life*, March 2009.

Read, Gordon, *Lancashire History Makers*, EP Publishing, 1975.

Roby, John, *Traditions of Lancashire, Vols 1 & 2*, Sixth Edition, intro. by Milner, George, John Heywood, *c.* 1900.

Rosbottom, Ernest, *Burscough, The Story of an Agricultural Village*, Carnegie Publishing, 1994.

Rowse, A.L., *Bosworth Field & The Wars of the Roses*, Wordsworth Editions, 1998.

Salway, Peter, *The Oxford Illustrated History of Roman Britain*, Book Club Associates/Oxford University Press, 1993.

Slater, Michael, *Charles Dickens*, Yale University Press, 2009.

'Spartina', *Looking at North Lancashire*, Dalesman, 1971.

Stenton, Sir Frank, *Anglo-Saxon England, The Oxford History of England*, 3rd Edition, Oxford University Press, 1971.

Sterling, Jane, *Elizabethan and Jacobean Lancashire*, Dalesman, 1973.

Sterling, Jane, *The Jacobite Rebellions in Lancashire*, Dalesman, 1973.

Watson, J. Steven, *The Reign of George III, 1760-1815, The Oxford History of England*, Oxford University Press, 1960.

Wikimedia and Wikipedia.

Wilks, Brian, *The Brontës*, Hamlyn, 1975.

Wolstenholme, Gerry, *Really Lancashire*, May 1996.

Yates, George C., *Colonel Rosworm and the Siege of Manchester*, S.R. Publishers, 1971, reprint of *Bygone Lancashire*, Ernest Axon (ed), 1892.

INDEX

Accrington 158, 172, 174
Accrington Pals 172
Ackroyd, Peter 114
Adams, Henry 150
Aelle, King of Deira 24
Aethelbert, King of Kent 24
Aethelburga of Northumbria 24
Aethelfrith, King of Bernicia 24
Aethelred, King of Wessex 26
Aethelwald, King of Deira 25
Agricola, Julius 18
Ainsworth, W. Harrison 55, 112, 113-118
Aire-Calder Gap 23
Aire-Ribble Gap 23
Albert, Prince 124
Alcock, John 173
Alden, John 85
Alfred the Great, King of Wessex 26-27, 28
Altham 64
Amounderness 32, 33, 35, 38
Anderton, Sir Francis of Lostock 92, 94
Angles 20, 21, 23-25, 27, 32
Anne of Denmark 63, 65
Anne, Queen 89
Anti-Corn Law League 102, 109
Arkholme 35
Arkwright, Richard 131, 132-140, 141
Arthur, King 24
Asheby, William 64
Ashton-under-Lyne 106, 108, 148, 159
Aske, Robert 55
Aspin, Chris 155
Assheton, Ralph 71, 72, 74, 75, 78
Assheton, Sir Richard, of Middleton 53
Astley Bridge 172
Asturians 20
Athelstan 28
Atherstone 48

Axon, William E. A. 88, 95, 98, 130, 151

Bagley, Dr. J. J. 34
Bakewell, Derbyshire 139
Bamborough Castle 24, 25
Bamford, Samuel 106, 107
Banastre, Sir Adam 37
Bankes, Joyce 160
Bankes, Meyrick 160
Bankes' Pier 161
Bannockburn, Battle of 37
Barnet, Battle of 45
Barnet Heath, Battle of 44
Barnoldswick 175, 176
Bartle Hall 62
Barrowford 21, 157
Barrow-in-Furness 166, 168, 174, 176
barrows 15
Bath 18, 41
Bauwens, Lievin 151-152
Bedchamber Crisis 101
Belgium 51, 151
Belper, Derbyshire 135, 136
Bennett, Walter 26
Bentley's Miscellany 115, 116
Bernicia 24
Berwick-upon-Tweed 47, 110
Big Bang, The 7
Billinge Beacon 98
Billington 25
Birkenhead 149
Blackburn 19, 28, 33, 37, 59, 62, 70, 71, 73, 77, 81, 108, 112, 113, 124, 125, 126, 130, 148, 155, 156, 157, 174
Black Death 38
Blackley 90
Blackpool 112, 165, 169, 174
Blackstone Edge 156
Blanche, of Lancaster 38, 39
Blanketeers 106
Bleasdale 16, 34

blockade-running 149
Blore Heath, Battle of 43
Blundell, Nicholas, Little Crosby 94
Blundell, William 87
Boer War 169
Boleyn, Anne 54
Bolton 19, 35, 70, 71, 76, 80, 108,
  112, 124, 132, 135, 140, 141,
  142, 156, 158, 159, 161, 163,
  166, 172, 174
Bolton, Battle of 76
Bolton-by-Bowland 45
Bolton-le-Moors 57, 153
Book of Sports 63
Booth, Sir George 81
Bootle 98
Boroughbridge, Battle of 37
Boston Courier 150
Bosworth Field, Battle of 39, 49
Boteler, William 36
Boudica, Queen 17
Boulton and Watt 124, 139
Bowland 14, 113
Boyne, Battle of the 82
Brabantin de Nassau, Charlotte 74
Bradford, John 56
Bradshaw, Captain 68
Bradshaw, Mr., of Wigan 57
Brereton, Sir William 72
Bridgewater Canal 124, 158
Bridgewater, Duke of 158
Brief Encounter 177-178
Brierfield 155
Brigantes 16, 18
Bright, John 100, 102, 109, 148
Brindley, James 158
British Aerospace (BAE
  SYSYEMS) 175, 177
British Northrop looms 156
Brontë, Charlotte 110-112
Brontë, Patrick 110-111
Bronze Age 16
Broughton-in-Furness 102
Broughton, Sir Thomas 50
Brown, Arthur Whitten 173
Browne, Hablot Knight, 'Phiz' 115
Bruce, Robert the 37
Brun, River 28
Brunanburh 28
Brungerley 45
Buckingham, Lord 47
Burnley 28, 35, 63, 70, 72, 77, 108,
  148, 154, 156, 158, 165, 172, 174

Burrow in Lonsdale 19
Burscough 15, 34, 42, 55, 158, 159
Bury 69, 71, 124, 128, 142, 148,
  156, 157, 159
Butler, Richard, of Rawcliffe Hall
  90
Buxton 17, 156
Byrom, John 95, 96, 97

Cadwallon, King of Gwynedd 24
Caesar, Julius 17
Calder, River 23, 70, 77, 78, 111
Camp Hill 16
canals 157-159
Canute 9
Cape Cod 84
Cape of Good Hope 167
Carboniferous period 13, 14
Carlisle 19, 62, 65, 65, 97
Carnforth 16, 177-178
Carpenter, General 91, 93
Cartmel 16, 33, 34, 35, 55, 73
Cartwright, Edmund 123, 138, 144
Carver, Stephen 117, 118
Castercliffe 16, 21, 22, 153
Castlehead 16
Castlestede 16
Catherine of Valois, wife of Henry
  V 42, 46
Catholics 55, 56, 60, 62, 66, 67, 82,
  86, 89, 90, 92, 94
Central Lancashire League, cricket
  174
Celts 16, 22, 23, 24
Chadderton 175
Channel Tunnel Co. 165
Charles I, King 66, 67, 69-79
Charles II, King 79-82
Charnock Richard 35
Charlotte de Tremouille,
  Countess of Derby 67, 74, 80, 81
Charteris, Colonel, of Hornby
  Castle 91
Chartists 108
Cheeryble Brothers 112
chemical industry 119, 155
Cheshire 32, 33, 41, 45, 46, 48, 57,
  73, 79, 81, 119, 147, 155
Chester 19, 24, 27, 41, 53, 57, 76,
  79, 80
Chetham Society 58
Childwall 53
Chippenham, Wiltshire 27

Chisnall, Captain Edward 75
Chorley 37, 49, 79, 124, 125, 131,
    135, 148, 171, 172
Chorley, Richard, of Chorley 92
Chowbent 70, 92, 135
Christianity 21, 24, 25, 27, 28, 29
Christian, William 82
Christmas Carol, A 112
Churchill, Winston 108
Civil War, American 146-151
Civil Wars, English 66-80, 89
Clarke, Fred, and the *Titanic* 170
Claudius, Emperor 17
Clifford, Lady Margaret 57, 58
Clifton 73
Clifton, Colonel 76
Clifton, Sir Thomas 87
Clitheroe 22, 35, 36, 37, 45, 63, 77,
    78, 81, 104, 108, 147, 156, 175
Clitheroe Castle 35, 37, 77, 79
Cliviger 14
coal industry 57, 119, 153-155,
    166, 173
Cobden, Richard 102, 109
Cockerham 34
Cockersand 34
Colne 16, 21, 37, 63, 70, 73, 77,
    153, 158, 164, 170, 175
Conishead 34, 71
Constantine, Emperor 21
Constantine, Learie, cricketer
    174-175
Continental drift 12
Coppock, Thomas 97
Corn Laws, Repeal of 101, 109,
    164
Cottom, John 59, 60
Cotton is King 146
Cotton Famine, the 146-151
cotton industry, history of 57, 199-
    152, 167, 168, 173
cotton, Surat 147
Cowan Bridge school 111
Cranford 110
Craven 77
Cricket 194
Crawford, Sir James 152
    Crimean War 102, 104
Cromford, Derbyshire 134, 135,
    136, 139
Crompton, Samuel 131, 138, 140-
    146
Cromwell, Oliver 75-78, 81

Cromwell, Thomas 55
Crosby 28, 94, 171
Cross, Richard Assheton, Viscount
    100, 102
Cross Street Chapel, Manchester
    90, 110
Croston 35
Cruikshank, George 115
Cuerdale Hoard 28
Culloden 97
Cumberland 33, 34, 37, 45, 77,
    90, 166
Cumberland, Duke of 96, 97
Cumbrians 28
Cunobelinus 17
Cyanobacteria 10

Daemonologie 63
Daglish, Robert, of Orrell 161
Dale, David 138
Dalton-in Furness 35
Dalton, John, of Thurnham Hall
    90, 93
Danegeld 29
Danelaw 27, 28, 29
Danes 25-31
Darwen 113, 126
David I, King of Scotland 35
Deepdale, Preston 37
Deira 24, 25
de Lacy, Alice 37
de Lacy, Henry 34
de Lacy, John 36
de Lacy, Roger 35
Deane 56
Denmark 25, 26, 29, 63
Derby, Charles, 8th Earl 80
Derby, Edward, 3rd Earl 54-57
Derby, Edward, 13th Earl 144, 145
Derby, Edward, 14th Earl 103, 151
Derby, Edward, 15th Earl 101
Derby, Edward, 17th Earl 173
Derby, Ferdinando, 5th Earl 58, 61
Derby, Henry, 4th Earl 57, 58, 61
Derby, James, 7th Earl 67-80
Derby, 9th Earl 92
Derby, The, horse race 77
Derby, Thomas, 1st Earl 39, 43, 47,
    48, 49, 52
Derby, Thomas, 2nd Earl 54
Derby, Twelfth Earl 77
Derby, William, 6th Earl 58
Derwent, River 134, 135

Derwentwater, Earl of 90, 93
Dicconson, William 87
Dickens, Charles 111, 112-118, 165
Dinosaurs, extinction of 12
Disraeli, Benjamin 102, 103
Dodding, Colonel George, of Conishead Priory 71
Dolby, George 112
Domesday Book 32, 33
Doncaster 41
Douglas, River 158
Downham 77, 177
Dublin 28
Durham 32, 102, 161
Duxbury, family 49
Duxbury, Massachusetts 84, 85

Earby 26
Earth, birth of 10
East Angles 25
East Anglia 26, 27, 28, 47
East India Co. 57, 121, 167
East Lancashire Railway 164
East Midlands 26, 27
Eccles 163
Eccleston, Thomas 87
Edenfield 157
Edge, Captain Oliver 80
Edgehill (Oxfordshire), Battle of 70
Edinburgh 64, 65, 96
Edmund, St., King of East Anglia 28
Edmund Crouchback 36
Edmund, Duke of York 39, 40, 41
Edmund Ironside 29
Edward I, King 35, 36
Edward II, King 37
Edward III, King 38, 39
Edward IV, King 38, 44-47
Edward V, Prince, killed in the Tower 47
Edward VI, King 56
Edward VII, King 169, 170
Edward VIII, abdication of 175
Edward, Prince of Wales, son of Henry VI 44, 45, 46
Edward, the Black Prince 38, 39
Edward the Confessor 29, 31, 33
Edward the Elder, King of Wessex 27
Edwin, King of Northumbria 24
Elizabeth I, Queen 56, 57, 58, 83

Elizabeth II, Queen 38
Elizabeth of York, 47, 50
Elslack 19
Eric of Hlathir, of Northumbria 29
Erratics 14, 15
Espinasse, Francis 132, 134, 140
Ethelfleda of Mercia 28
Ethelred II, the Unready 29, 31

Fairfax, Sir Thomas 70, 73, 77, 78
Falkowski, Paul 10
Farmer, Captain William 75
Farrington, William, of Werden 75
ferries, L&YR 165
Fishwick, Colonel Henry 88
flints 15, 16, 22
Fleet debtors' prison 62
Fleet, Fred, and the Titanic 171
Fleetwood 19, 163, 164, 165
Fleetwood, Sir Peter Hesketh 163
flying shuttle 122, 128, 132, 138, 152
Football League 174
Formby 16, 28, 98
Forster, General 92, 93
Forster, John 112, 115, 116, 117
Foulridge 158
Fox, Richard 75
France 28, 41, 42, 44, 45, 47, 53, 54, 80, 82, 87, 89, 96, 97, 107, 129, 152
Freckleton 176-177
Fullwood 34, 67
Furness 13, 14, 33, 34, 35, 37, 45, 51, 55, 73
Fylde 73

Galgate 19
Gamel, thegn, of Rochdale 33
Gandhi, Mahatma 126
Garstang 38, 49, 78, 91, 93, 159
Gaskell, Mrs Elizabeth Cleghorn 109-110, 112
General Strike (1926) 173
geology 13-14
George I, King 89, 92, 93
George II, King 96, 98
George III, King 98
George IV, King 99
George V, King 170, 175
George VI, King 175
George, Duke of Clarence 46
George Silverman's Explanation 113

Georgiana, Duchess of Devonshire 139
Gerrard, Sir Gilbert 68
Gerrard, Thomas 87
Gerrard, Sir William, of Bryn 87, 88
Gerrard, Lord, of Ashton Hall 62
Ghent, Belgium 38
Gilbert, James, railway map 163
Girlington, Lady 70
Girlington, Sir John 67, 68, 71, 73
Gisburn 78
glaciation 11, 14, 15
Gladstone, William Ewart 100, 103, 104, 149, 165, 167
Glendower, Owen 41
Glorious Revolution 82, 86
Godwine, Earl, of Wessex 29
Great Central Railway 164
Great Depression, 1930's 173
Great Stone of Fourstones 15
Green, Alexander 68
Greenhalgh Castle 73, 78
Grelley, Robert 36
Grey, Earl 103, 108
Grey, Lady Jane 56, 107, 108

Hadrian's Wall 19
Haggate 77
Haigh 153
Halifax 163
Halle, Charles 110
Hall i'th' Wood, Bolton 140, 142
Hamburg 152
Hamilton, Duke of 78, 79
Harald Hardrada, King of Norway 30
Hard Times 112
Hargreaves, James 124, 129-132, 133, 134, 137
Harold, King of England 29-31
Harold Harefoot 29
Harper, Amanda 139
Harrington, John 44, 54
Harrington, Sir Thomas 43, 44
harrying of the North, the (1069) 32
Harthacnut, son of Canute 29
Hartley, Wallace Henry, and the *Titanic* 170
Harvey, William 66
Haslingden 148, 156
Hastings, Battle of 30

Hastings, Lord 47
Hawks House, Reedley 79
Haworth 111, 112
Hay, Rev. W. R. 106, 107
Henrietta Maria, Queen 67, 73
Henry I, King 35
Henry II, King 36
Henry III, King 36, 40
Henry IV, King, Bolingbroke 40, 41
Henry V, King 41, 42
Henry VI, King 42, 43-46, 47
Henry VI (Shakespeare) 61
Henry VII, King, Henry Tudor 46, 47, 48, 49, 50-53, 58
Henry VIII, King 20, 53-55
Henry, Duke of Lancaster 38
Hesketh, Gabriel, of Whitehill, Goosnargh 92
Hesketh, Richard, of Rufford 58
Hexham 24, 45
Heysham 28
Highs, Thomas, of Leigh 131, 133, 137
Hill, Lawrence 40
Hodder, River 78
Hodgson, Albert 90, 94
Hoghton, Alexander, of Lea 59
Hoghton, Lady 70
Hoghton, Sir Gilbert 70
Hoghton, Sir Henry 91, 92, 96
Hoghton, Richard 62
Hoghton, Thomas 59, 62
Hoghton Tower 59, 62, 71, 112, 113, 114
Holcombe Hill 102
Holden, Anthony 59
Holdsworth, Jonas 170
Holland, Robert 37
Hollinfare 158
Holy Island 26
Honorius, Emperor 22
Horik, King of Denmark 26
Hornby 35, 36, 44, 51, 53, 54, 62, 73, 91
Hoyle, Sir Fred 7
Hubble, Edwin 8
Huddersfield 159
Huddlestone, Colonel, of Millom 73
Hunt, Henry, "Orator" 107
Huskisson, William 162, 163
Ice Age 11
Ilkley 19, 22

India 121, 124, 125, 126, 141, 142, 143, 147, 164, 167
industrial espionage 151-152
Ireland 26, 35, 40, 43, 50, 51, 72, 82, 166, 168, 173
Ireland, Thomas, of Bewsey Hall 62
Irish Sea 26, 158
Iron Age 16, 22
Irwell, River 157, 158
Isle of Sheppey, Kent 26
Isle of Man 26, 41, 57, 73, 74, 76, 78, 79, 81
Ismay, Joseph Bruce 171

Jack Sheppard 116, 117
Jacobites 66, 87, 90
Jacobite Rebellion (1715) 89-94
Jacobite Rebellion (1745) 96-97
James I of England, VI of Scotland 52, 62-66, 75, 112, 113, 114
James IV, King of Scotland 52
James II, King 82, 86, 87, 89
Jane Eyre 111
John, King 35, 36
John of Gaunt 38, 39, 46

Kay, John, and flying shuttle 122, 124, 127-129, 132, 138
Kay, John, of Leigh 131, 133, 134, 137
Kay-Shuttleworth, Sir James 110, 111, 112, 151
Kendal 159
Kennedy, Jane 63
Kennedy, John 143, 145
Kenny, Annie 108
Kensal Green, London 118
Kenyon, James 152
Kirkby Lonsdale 19, 91, 111
Kirkham 19, 73, 132
Knighting of the loin 113-114, 115
Knowsley 41, 59, 80
Knutsford, Cheshire 110

Lake District 13, 29
Lambert, Sir John, Major General 79
Lancashire and Yorkshire Railway 164, 165
Lancashire, East 33, 37, 63, 70, 73, 76, 111, 125, 157, 174
Lancashire League, cricket 174
Lancashire Plot, The 86-88

Lancashire Witch, steam engine 161
Lancashire Witches, The 55, 113, 114, 117, 118
Lancaster 15, 16, 19, 34, 35, 36, 37, 38, 55, 56, 57, 62, 64, 70, 71, 72, 83, 88, 90, 91, 92, 93, 96, 97, 105, 106, 108, 112, 156, 163
Lancaster Canal 159
Langdale, Sir Marmaduke 77, 78
Langton, Philip 87
Latchford 18
Lathom 34, 41, 47, 52, 59, 60, 61, 62, 73-76, 79, 80
Lathom, Isabel 41
Lathom, Siege of 73-76
Lathom, Sir Thomas 41
Lawson, Robert 91
Layton Hawes, Bispham 73, 76
Lee, Ann 98-99
Leeds 25, 128, 163
Leeds-Liverpool Canal 158, 159, 160, 161
Lee, General Robert E. 151
Leicester 18, 27, 48
Leigh 131, 132, 133, 159, 161
Lelland, John 20, 57, 153
Levenshulme 68
Leybourn, John, of Nateby 92
Leyden 83
Leyland 73, 68
Lichfield, Diocese of 28, 55
Lightoller, Charles 171
Lilburne, Colonel Robert 79
Lincoln 17, 27
Lincoln, President Abraham 149
Lindale 16
Lindeth Tower, Silverdale 110
Lionel, Duke of Clarence 39, 43
Littleborough 19
Liverpool 16, 35, 36, 37, 56, 67, 68, 72, 73, 76, 77, 93, 97, 98, 103, 108, 112, 117, 148, 149, 156, 158, 159, 161, 164, 165, 166, 167, 170, 171, 173, 174, 176,
Liverpool and Manchester Railway 161, 162
Liverpool Castle 41, 77, 88
Lofthouse, Jessica 45, 178
London and North Western Railway 164
Longfellow, Henry Wadsworth 85

Longmate, Norman 150
Longridge 19
Lonsdale 19, 33, 36
Lord, Captain Stanley, of the *Titanic* 172
Lord Strange's Men 59
Ludlow Castle 47
Lune, River 24, 26, 37, 71, 73, 91
Lunt, John 87

Macbeth 65
Macclesfield 159
Mackintosh, Brigadier 90, 93
Macintosh, Charles 124
Maclise, Daniel 118
Macrone, John 115
Magna Carta 36
Malcolm, King of Scotland 36
Man, development of 12-13, 15-16
Manchester 19, 28, 36, 52, 57, 67, 68, 70-73, 76, 78, 81, 87-90, 92-98, 104-116, 118, 121, 124, 135, 137-139, 143, 144, 148, 150, 152, 156, 158, 159, 164-166, 173, 174, 176
Manchester Act 121, 134
Manchester Cathedral 46, 53
Manchester Daily Examiner and Times 150
Manchester Herald 105
Manchester Ship Canal 159, 174
Manchester Thinking Club 105
Marcus Aurelius, Emperor 20
Margaret, sister of Henry VIII 52, 62
Margaret Beaufort 46, 48
Margaret of Anjou, wife of Henry VI 44, 45, 4
Marsh, George 56
Marston Moor, Battle of 77
Mary, Queen 55-56, 57
Mary, Queen, wife of William III 82, 86, 89
Mary Queen of Scots 52, 56, 57, 62
Mary of Modena 82
Mayflower 40, 83
Meldrum, Sir John 76, 77
Mersey, River 18, 28, 32, 35, 52, 56, 149, 157, 158
Mesozoic period 14
Metrical Record, Aston's 94=
Middleham, Wensleydale 47
Middle Stone Age 15

Middleton 53, 71, 106
Midland Railway 164
Milford Haven 48
Mitton Hall 112
Molyneux, Caryll, Third Lord 87, 88
Molyneux, Lord 68-70, 73
Molyneux, Sir Richard, of Sefton 42
Molyneux, Sir William, of Sefton 53
Monk, General 81
Monton 90
Moore, John 67, 74, 75, 76
Moorwood, Helen 60
Moray, Earl of 37
Mordaunt, Colonel 136
Morecambe Bay 19, 34, 50, 56, 110, 164
Morgan, Colonel 74
Morte, Adam, Mayor of Preston 70
Mortimer's Cross, Battle of 44
Mosley, Sir Edward 68, 69
Mosley, Sir Oswald, of Ancoats Hall 95
Mount Badon (Mons Badonicus) 23
mule, Crompton's spinning 138, 139, 140-144
Mullins, Priscilla 85
Muncaster Castle 45
Myerscough 34, 62, 70, 113

Nantwich 73, 80, 81
Napoleonic Wars 105
Naseby, Battle of 78
Neanderthal man 15
Nelson 16, 21, 64, 66, 174, 175
Neolithic period 15
Netherlands 83
Nevin, Charles 126, 177
Newcomen steam engine 155
Newfoundland 173
Newgate controversy 117
New Lanark 138
New Stone Age 15
Newton-in-Makerfield 33
Newton-le-Willows 104, 108, 163
Nicholls, Rev. Arthur Bell 112
Normandy 31
Norris, Colonel, of Speke 72
Norris, family 56
Norris, Sir Henry, of Speke 53

Northampton 43, 78
Norsemen 25, 26, 28
Northern Ireland 121, 132, 165, 171
North Meols (Southport) 35, 98
Northumbria 24-29
Northumberland 41
Norway 25, 29, 30, 63
Nottingham 27, 48, 69, 130, 133, 139
Nowell, Roger, JP of Read Hall 64, 69
Nowell, Roger, Royalist 69, 70
Nussey, Ellen 110-111

Ogle, Captain Henry 75
Oldham 71, 99 106, 108, 109, 148, 154, 159, 174
O'Neill, John, of Low Moor 147
Ordovician period 13
Ormskirk 28, 35, 67, 78
Orrell 161
Orwell, George 161
Osric, King of Deira
Oswald, King of Northumbria 24
Oswaldtwistle 130
Oswestry, Shropshire 25
Oswine, King of Deira 25
Oswiu, King of Bernicia 25
Overborough 19
Over Darwen 145
Over Wyresdale 34
Owen, Robert 138

Padiham 64, 70, 72, 110, 111
Palmerston, Lord 104
Pangaea 12
Pankhurst, family 108
Parliament 36, 55, 57, 66, 67, 68, 104, 121, 134, 136, 144, 149
Parliamentarians 66, 67, 68
Paslew, John, Abbot of Whalley 55
Paul, Lewis 129, 133
Peasants' Revolt 40
Peel, Sir Robert senior 100, 124, 142, 144
Peel, Sir Robert junior, Prime Minister 100, 101, 103, 109, 162
Peel, Yates & Co., of Bury 142
Pemberton 53
Penda, King of Mercia 24, 25
Pendle 14, 23, 26, 34, 63, 70, 83, 98, 177

Pennines 14, 23, 24, 25, 26, 159
Penwortham 34, 37
Penzias, Arno 8
Peploe, Samuel, Bishop of Chester 92
Percival, Richard 68
Percival, Spencer 144, 145
Percy 41
Peterloo Massacre 107
Phillip of Spain 57
Picts 22
Piel of Fouldray 50, 56
Pilgrimage of Grace 54-55
Pilling 53
Plymouth 84
Pontefract Castle 37, 41, 47
population 34, 57, 105, 166, 168
Portfield 16
Potter, Beatrix 110
Poulton-le-Fylde 15, 53
Presbyterianism 78, 79, 82
Prescot 155, 156
Preston 19, 28, 35-38, 53, 57, 59, 60, 62, 67, 68, 70, 71, 72, 74, 78, 79, 91, 92, 93, 96, 97, 102, 108, 112, 113, 125, 132, 133, 148, 156, 157, 159, 163, 165, 166, 174, 175, 176
Preston, Battle of 78
Prestonpans, Battle of 96
Prestwich 149
Pudsay, Sir Ralph 45
Puritans 66, 67, 71, 81, 83

Queen's Players 58, 65
Queen Street Mill, Burnley 127
Quernmore 34

Radcliffe, Captain 68, 75
railways 160-165
Rainhill Trials 162
Ramsbottom 100, 102
Ravenspur, Yorkshire 40
Rawlinson, Robert 150
Rawsthorne, Captain Edward 75
Read Bridge 72
Reading 26
Reform Act (1832) 104-109
Reform Act (1867) 103, 108, 149
Restoration, the, 81
Ribble, River 16, 20, 23, 24, 26, 28, 30, 32, 33, 35, 36, 45, 92, 113, 158, 159, 176

Ribblesdale 14, 72, 73, 77, 93
Ribbleton Moor 78
Ribchester 19, 20, 21, 22, 37, 53
Ribchester hoard 21
Richard I, King, the Lionheart 36
Richard II, King 38, 39, 40
Richard III, King (Duke of
  Gloucester) 46-49
Richard III (Shakespeare) 61
Richard, Duke of Normandy 29, 31
Richard, Duke of York 43
Richard, Duke of York, son of
  Edward VI 47
Ricsige, King of Northumbria 27
Rigby, Colonel Alexander 67, 70,
  73, 74, 76
Riley, Dr., Portsmouth 119
Rising in the North (1569) 56
Rivers, Lord 68
Robert, Lord of Lathom 34
Roberts, Richard 143
Robinson, Edmund 65, 66
Roby, John 45, 54, 55
Rochdale 33, 34, 35, 53, 71, 102,
  106, 107, 108, 109, 148, 156,
  157, 159, 174
Rochdale Society of Equitable
  Pioneers 109
Rocket, Stephenson's 162, 163
Roger de Montbegon 36
Roger de Poitou 34, 35
Rolls-Royce 175, 176
Romans 17-22, 153
Roman withdrawal 22, 23
Rookwood 115, 116, 117, 118
Roscoe, William, and slavery 167
Rossall Point 79
Rossendale 14
Roston, Capt. A.H. 172
Rosworm, Colonel 68, 73
Royalists 67, 68
Rufford 58, 60, 158
Runcorn 158, 159
Rupert, Prince 75, 76, 77
Rushen Castle, Isle of Man 73, 82

Sabden Brook 72
St Albans, Battle of 39, 43
St Annes 165
St Helens 154, 158
St Michael's on Wyre 73
Salford 33, 35, 51, 68, 73, 107,
  108, 148, 156, 158, 166, 176

Samlesbury 175
Sankey Canal 158
Sarmatians 20
Savannah, the 149
Saxons 21, 22, 23-25, 26, 27, 28,
  29, 31, 33
Scarisbrick 159
Scotland 24, 26, 35, 36, 37, 41, 44,
  47, 53, 55, 62, 63, 64, 67, 78, 79,
  90, 96, 110, 113, 164
Scots 22, 28
Scott, Sir Walter 53
Scrope, Baron 59, 64
Seaton, Sir John, Major General
  70, 71
Sefton 53
Shaftesbury, Lord 149
Shakers 98
Shakespeare, William 17, 49,
  58-61, 65
Shap Fells 163, 164
Sheffield 164
Sherburne, Sir Nicholas 87
Shrewsbury 41, 48, 69
Shuttleworth, Sir Richard 67, 70,
  72, 73, 76-79
Silurian period 13
Silverdale 110
Simnel, Lambert 50-51
Simon de Montfort 36
Skelmore Head 16
Skipton 37, 77, 164
slavery 103, 104, 146, 148, 149,
  166
Smalley, John, of Preston 133, 135
Solar system, development of 10
Southampton 83, 148, 170
Southerns, Elizabeth, Old Demdike
  64
Southport 151, 159, 169, 174
Southworth, Sir John, of
  Samlesbury 56
Spanish Armada 56
Speedwell 83
spinning-jenny, Hargreaves' 124,
  130-131, 134, 140, 141, 143,
  144, 145, 152
Stair, Earl of 90
Stamford Bridge, Battle of 30
Standedge Tunnel 159
Standishes of Duxbury 83
Standishes of Standish 40, 68
Standish, Myles 83-85

Standish, Ralph, of Standish 92, 94
Standish, Thomas, of Duxbury 68
Standish, William 87
Stanley, Sir Edward, Lord
  Monteagle 52-54
Stanley, George 51
Stanley, Sir John 41, 42
Stanley, Sir Roland 87
Stanley, Sir Thomas 39, 42
Stanley, Sir William 39, 43, 48,
  51, 52
Stanlow, Cheshire 34
Starkey, Captain 71
Starkie, Nicholas 96
Stephen, King 34, 35
Stephenson, George 161, 162, 163
Stoneyhurst 78
Strathclyde 24
Stretford 158
Strutt, Jedediah, of Derby 133, 136
Stuart, Charles Edward, the
Young Pretender, Bonnie Prince
Charlie 94-97
Stuart, James Edward, the Old
Pretender 89, 91, 94
Sussex 17, 30
Swarkestone Bridge, Derby 97
Sydall, Thomas 90, 91, 93
Sydall, Thomas, the younger 97

Talbot, family 39, 45, 48
Tamworth Manifesto 101
Tempest, family 45
Tewkewsbury, Battle of 46
Thackeray, William Makepiece 115
Thelwall 28
Thomas, Earl of Lancaster 37
Thurland Castle 72
The Times 107, 146, 147, 15
Titanic, the 170-172
Toleration Act (1689) 89
Tostig 29, 30, 32
Tower of London 40, 45, 46, 47,
  50, 51
Towneley, Charles 70
Towneley, Francis, Colonel 96, 97
Towneley, Sir John 97
Towneley, Richard 92, 94
Townson, Mr., of Lancaster 71
Towton, Battle of 44, 45
Toxteth 34
Trawden 34
Tremouille, Duke de 74

Trent incident, the 148
Trent, River 25, 97
Tudor, Edmund 48
Tudor, Jasper 44, 46, 48
Tudor, Owen 42, 44, 46
Tunstall, family 45
Turner, John, of Preston 92
Turnpike Trusts 156
Turpin, Dick 115, 117
Tyldesley, Edward, of Myerscough
  90
Tyldesley, Sir Thomas, of
  Myerscough 68, 70, 73, 76, 78, 79
Tyler, Wat 40

Ulverston 16, 35
United States 112, 115, 123, 146,
  166, 167, 172, 176-177
Up Holland 37, 55, 78

Victoria, Queen 99, 100, 104, 124,
  169
Vikings 25-31
volcanic activity 11, 13

Waddington 45
Wade, General 96, 97
Wakefield, Battle of 44
Wales 18, 24, 25, 27, 35, 36, 41,
  44, 46, 48
Walker Art Gallery, Liverpool 118
Walker, Thomas 105
Wallace, William 36
Walmersby, Bury 127
Walmsley, Bartholomew 87, 88
Walton Bridge 78, 92
Walton, John, of Horwich 92
Walton-le-Dale 35, 90, 92
Warbeck, Perkin 50-53
Warrington 28, 33, 34, 35, 36, 49,
  52, 53, 62, 67, 69, 70, 72, 74, 78,
  79, 81, 86, 96, 108, 110, 137,
  156, 163
Wars of the Roses 38-49
Warton Crag 98
Warton, North Lancashire 16, 35, 53
Warton, Preston 175, 176-177
Warwick, Earl of 43, 44, 45, 46
water-frame, Arkwright's 134, 138,
  141, 143, 144, 145
Watkin, Absalon 164
Watkin, Sir Edward William 164,
  165

Watling Street 19
Wedacre 53
Wellington, Duke of 100, 107, 108,
  162, 163
Wenning, River 26
Wessex 26-29
West Derby 33, 34, 77
Westhoughton 173
West Indies 93, 148, 166, 167
Westmorland 33, 34, 77, 78, 90,
  158
Whalley 16, 25, 26, 34, 55, 63, 70,
  72, 112, 165, 174
Wharton, Lord 67
White Star Line 170, 171
Whitney, Eli, saw gin 123
Whittaker, John, of Wigan, 147
Widnes 37
Wigan 19, 35-37, 53, 57, 70-74,
  78, 79, 93, 96, 108, 124, 125,
  148, 153, 156-161, 163, 166, 174
Wigan Lane, Battle of 79
Wigan Pier 161
Wilberforce, William 146
Willersley Castle, Derbyshire 136,
  139
William I, the Conqueror 30, 31, 35
William II, Rufus 35
William III, of Orange 82, 86, 87,
  89
William IV, King 99, 108
Wills, General 92, 93
Wilson, Robert 8
Winstanley 160
Winwick Green 78
Wirral Peninsula 29
Wolsey, Cardinal 54
Woods, Rev. James, of Chowbent
  92
Woollen industry, 57, 121, 129, 130
Worcester, 79, 80
Worcester, Battle of, 80
First World War, 125, 155, 169,
  171, 172-175
Second World War, 127, 175-8
Worsley, 124, 158
Worsley, Colonel, of Manchester, 8
Wycoller, 21, 37, 111
Wyre, River, 19, 71, 79

Yates, Peter 178
Yates, William, 98
York, 24, 26, 55, 115

Yorkshire, 7, 15, 26, 27, 32, 33, 37,
  38, 45, 55, 64, 70, 72, 73, 77, 78,
  81, 111, 124, 130, 156, 159, 164,
  165, 166, 174, 175
Young, Arthur, 157